The Family of
GURU ST K.P.
PANGGABEAN

The Bible Story is the truth
God made a covenant with His servant

Miniature Israel In The Gentile

BINSAR PANGGABEAN

Inks and Bindings
888-290-5218
www.inksandbindings.com
orders@inksandbindings.com

Contents

The Family of Guru St K.P. Panggabean: Miniature Israel in the Gentile

An Overview of the book

"The Family of Guru St K.P. Panggabean: Miniature Israel in the Gentile" is a captivating memoir of the author's family history, shared by his parents and guided by divine inspiration. Through spiritual insights and profound revelations, the book explores the author's father's divine calling, the hardships faced by the family, the author's own individual journey, and the tasks assigned to the whole family. The author set the book to serve as a testimony of his deep spiritual reflection to his divine personal and family calling and his realization of the parallels between his family's story and the Scriptures.

The author, guided by The Holy Spirit, unfolds his family's past, seeking a deeper understanding of his father's calling, through the experiences and inter-relationship between the family with his relatives and neighbors. Through moments of reflection, spiritual guidance, and encounters with God in Theophany, visions and dreams, the author is compelled to document the remarkable events that have shaped his family's journey.

At the heart of the story is St. KP Panggabean, the author's father, who was called by God to leave his homeland and venture to the Promised Land to establish a church. Filled with unwavering faith and devotion, St. KP Panggabean triumphs over numerous tests and trials, while he is fulfilling his divine calling, until he is witnessing the fulfillment of God's promises through physical blessings, e.g: daily food, basic needs, the conquest of the Promised Lands, and the birth of his children and grandchildren; and also including through the spiritual blessings and achievement with glorious moments, a meeting with God the Almighty in his last days; e.g: theophany, vision and dreams.

The author uses the personal experiences of his family in order to provide evidence of the authenticity and relevance of the stories found in the Bible. It aims to dispel doubts and skepticism by demonstrating that the Bible contains true accounts that are not merely humanly crafted fairy tales. The book serves as a powerful testimony to the existence of God and His ongoing work in the lives of contemporary individuals with the same pattern, namely covenant relationship.

By intertwining personal narratives, spiritual revelations, and the timeless truths of Scripture, "The Family of Guru St K.P. Panggabean" offers a compelling exploration of faith, divine calling, and the remarkable ways in which God continues to work in the lives of ordinary people with typical pattern of God's frame work, that is a covenant friendship. It invites readers who struggle with belief in biblical stories to reconsider and embrace the profound reality of God's presence and his transformative power in the modern world.

In summary, this memoir presents a thought-provoking account of the author's family, highlighting their spiritual journey and the undeniable parallels between their modern daily lives and the prophetic stories found in the Bible. It serves as an affirmation of God's existence and his continued involvement in the lives of individuals today, offering readers a renewed sense of faith and an appreciation for the living narratives contained within sacred texts. The clue is: if you follow what the Bible says to you, you may find the same extraordinary events as the Bible unfolds it to you. If you install true worship to God, do good to Him as well as to man, strictly obey God's law, walk before Him and be blameless, you will be awarded glorious crown by Him at the end of your life.

CHAPTER ONE

The Formation Of The Family

Ge 32:24 So Jacob was left alone, and a man wrestled with him till daybreak. When the man saw that he could not overpower him, he touched the socket of Jacob's hip so that his hip was wrenched as he wrestled with the man. Then the man said, "Let me go, for it is daybreak." But Jacob replied, "I will not let you go unless you bless me." The man asked him, "What is your name?" "Jacob," he answered. Then the man said, **"Your name will no longer be Jacob, but Israel**, because you have struggled with God and with men and have overcome."

I n year 1908, when Indonesia was under the occupation of the Dutch government, St Cyrus Panggabean was born. St Cyrus, granddad, was live in Pansurnapitu. But He moves with his wife, Esmeria to Angkola. In Angkola Esmeria gave birth Karmel at 13*th* September 1935. Then they move back to Pansurnapitu. In Pansurnapitu, Esmeria gave birth to Ready at 30 October 1940. So that St Cyrus has two children, one son and one daughter. St Cyrus was prophesying to his children that ia hamu iananghonku holan dua do hamuna songon pat ni manuk. You both are my children which like rooster that has two legs. Molo ponggol sada ndang boi I mardalan dohot denggan. If one of its legs broke, then the rooster will not walk properly. Jadi masiurupan ma hamu. Thus both of you had to help each other. They have eight separate lands in Pansurnapitu consist of: five small paddy fields: toru ni dalan Tagambing in front of granddad house, Tapus, Sisira, Parsamasi, Hitihorbo (near Tarutung market); 1 small land for vegetation and cage for pigs, 1 land for three small houses in Tagahambing, and one land outside Pansurnapitu in the jungle which planted with myrrh tree and named Horsik. They have water well besides their home. St Cyrus, granddad, said that there was thick rain and storm and thunder and suddenly a fountain comes out besides his house. St Cyrus was an elder in the Church Pansurnapitu and Esmeria involved in woman ministry. The Church Pansurnapitu was the fruit of the German evangelist name Ludwig Ingwer Nommensen, who came to Tarutung and blessed the village in a mount name Mount Cross of Love. The evangelists who assigned to continue the evangelization were Pieter Johansen and his wife and the other evangelists. In 4 July 1960 Karmel get married with Ruslan in Butar. The biblical reference at the wedding ceremonial in the Church was taken from Gen.32:24. The pastor preached that family problems are some kind like a struggle of Jacob, or Israel. Mrs. Ruslan was prophesying the passage for several times in the family gathering, in the family celebration or in the hardest time. The author thought this prophesying was only a sweet taste of word in an oracle and did not have any signification and meaning for our life. But as the time goes by he understands it was a prophesying. It is not like a new revelation from a new prophet, but the story of the Old covenant and New covenant revelation were retold and reminded by a prophet. Prophet that proclaim remind and retell the God's covenant and law to his people that have been revealed in the Bible. After two years marriage, a beauty daughter was born and St Cyrus and his wife Esmeria named their grandchild Boaz, but Karmel and Ruslan named her Theo. Prinsloo said that human action sometimes even replaces divine action; however they were limited and futile without divine blessing or action (1980, 339). And God had sovereignly determined His divine election and grace to call Abraham to a covenant friendship out from his father homeland into a promised land and blessed him to be blessed for the world. We are, who were originally the Gentiles, grafted into the heritage of Abraham, the olive tree, because we have confess Jesus Christ as our savior and we enjoy the benefit of God's promises and heirs of God's covenantal promises down through our generations. The pruning principle or cut-off or ex-communicate of the ethnical Jews are those who were not heirs of God's promises to Abraham, due to their unfaithfulness unto covenant of God. But the Gentiles and Jews who believe in Christ will be grafted in the olive tree, the New Israel. The covenantal friendship that He wants to establish with Abraham is a bond in blood sovereignly administered by God (O.P. Robertson, 1980, 4). A bond in blood means that covenant relationship is demands a life and death issue. If Abram would have reject God's "offer" of covenant with him, he would die. It costs the death as well for the party who unfaithful to the covenant friendship. It is demand a continual faithfulness in both parties throughout their descendants. Both parties, God and Abraham and his descendants, should be commits to the covenant because it is tying them. A commitment to obey God from man's party; and blessing from God's party. The covenant indeed was personal union and friendship with God into a life of obedience, to follow and to obey Him in holiness of life (Joseph Morecraft III, Covenant lectures). .

CHAPTER TWO

The Call Of Abram

Ge 11:28 While his father Terah was still alive, Haran died in Ur of the Chaldeans, in the land of his birth. Abram and Nahor both married. The name of Abram's wife was Sarai, and the name of Nahor's wife was Milcah; she was the daughter of Haran, the father of both Milcah and Iscah. Now Sarai was barren; she had no children. Terah took his son Abram, his grandson Lot son of Haran, and his daughter-in-law Sarai, the wife of his son Abram, and together they set out from Ur of the Chaldeans to go to Canaan.

Ge 12:1-5 The LORD had said to Abram, "**Leave your country, your people and your father's household and go to the land I will show you.** "I will make you into a great nation and I will bless you; I will make your name great, and you will be a blessing. I will bless those who bless you, and whoever curses you I will curse; and all peoples on earth will be blessed through you." So Abram left, as the LORD had told him; and **Lot went with him. Abram was seventy-five years old when he set out from Haran. He took his wife Sarai, his nephew Lot**, all the possessions they had accumulated and the people they had acquired in

Haran, and they set out for the land of Canaan, and they arrived there. *Ge 12:7* The LORD appeared to Abram and said, "To your offspring I will give this land." So **he built an altar there to the LORD, who had appeared to him. *Ge 12:10* Now there was a famine in the land, and Abram went down to Egypt to live there for a while because the famine was severe.**

In year around 1964-1965 **there was a severe famine in Indonesia** at the edge of the fall of the reign of President Soekarno. The people suffered enormously as hyperinflation exceeding 600% per annum, and everywhere they have to queuing to buy food. The economical crisis and social situation became worse whenever October 1, 1965, at the break of day, the pro-communist "30 September Movement" revolt and claimed that it acted to protect President Soekarno from an impending army coup. The government even cannot pay states employee.

Karmel was born at September 9, 1935. He was lived in a small village named Pansunapitu, huta Tagahambing, with his wife, and the firstborn daughter and their parents there at severe social-economical situation. He was a state teacher on the district town, Tarutung. The severe economical crisis at 1965 resulted to his family. He was not received salary from the Government for three months. He, then not work and thus he had no money for his family even though he lives with his parents. He stays at home and gathered with his friend in a shop or 'lapo' (a shop which sells tuak, traditional alcohol, and a host to play card or chess) in his idle time. They were also asked God to give to them a son to continue family of his father line.

Three months before Christmas in 1965 on Sunday morning, the whole family went to the Church. At the pulpit, his father, St. Cyrus Panggabean an elder in the Church, was in duty to preach. He preached the Abraham Calling as per Church almanac. Perhaps because of his father was in duty in the pulpit, **Karmel likes the preaching and response to the God's calling as Abraham did: Yes, Dear God, I want to obey your calling** (but of course this within his deep heart only). Then comes Christmas season the times to celebrate with new dress for his daughter. But He had no money and asked his mother, grandma to borrow her money to buy new dress for her grand-girl. Despite he had money to borrow, grandma suspected him to have play card and gambling in the coffee shop or lapo. She had been told that dad did not have the salary for three months, but she doesn't understand. And she raises in angry and shout **to send away** dad from her house. She shouts with a loud voice: **"laho ma ho!" (You go away)"**. Dad response her without any doubt and fear with the loud voice as well: **"ba laho ma ahu!" (Yes, I will go)**. This historical event was kept in mind by mom and told in the family gathering or celebration for several times as testimony or even prophecy. When this happened she feels this is unfortunate event for her family, but latter when her husband passed away she feels that this event is a blessing to her family, that her husband sent away by God to found a church and receive the Promised Lands, and the promised sons and grandsons.

Now the family lives in a small rent house in the same village. Thus after discussion with his wife, he decided to go to Jakarta, our capital city to find work there. They were planned to move with his wife and the firstborn daughter right after he find the work. Shortly, dad went to Jakarta and find mom's sister. He lives in their house for about 3 months and her husband help him to find the job as a private school teacher. Right after he gets the job, then mom and the firstborn daughter went to Jakarta. They were live in a small rent house that had no bathroom and the roof is leaking, and without floor. When rain comes down the roof is leaking and water filled the land that makes wet around the house. For this suffering, the firstborn daughter said in sadness and cry: "mulak ma hita tu huta" (let's return to our country). This was the first test of Karmel in his calling. But they remain suffer that they asked God to open mom's womb and gave birth to a son to continue the family line. Mom was visit the main hospital in Jakarta to have a treatment. Mom was also promised to God that her son will be given to God to be a pastor. This was the second test to dad calling.

Then God remembered mom and opened her womb, pregnant and give birth to a son. They named him August. Granddad then came to visit them and take a photo. In other occasion, Grandma visited them and took a photo as well. They were happy that they have a son now. Even though the baby had a handicap due to the baby hard to pull away from the womb, then the sister pull it by her hands. One year after that, She conceived again and gave birth to a daughter named Ani. Thus August and Ani were born on that rented house.

A couple month later, a relative came visit them and advised dad to buy a land in Pulomas. Then he bought it and built a small house using used roof material from our relative and they give the bed for the family as well. Now Karmel has nine lands including one in Jakarta and eight in his father homeland.

> *Ge 29:31* **When the LORD saw that Leah …, he opened her womb**, … *Ge 29:32* **Leah became pregnant and gave birth to a son.** She named him **Reuben,** … *Ge 29:33* **She conceived again, and when she gave birth to a son** …So she named him **Simeon**. *Ge 29:34* **Again she conceived, and when she gave birth to a son** … So he was named **Levi.** *Ge 29:35* **She conceived again, and when she gave birth to a son she said, "This time I will praise the LORD."** So she named him **Judah.** *Ge 30:17* **God listened to Leah, and she became pregnant and bore Jacob a fifth son** *Ge 30:18* … So she named him **Issachar**. *Ge 30:19* **Leah conceived again and bore Jacob a sixth son.** *Ge 30:20* … So she named him **Zebulun.** *Ge 30:21* Sometime later she gave birth to a **daughter and named her Dinah.**

Then God remembered mom and opened her womb and became pregnant and give birth to a son. They named him August. After one year, She conceived again and gave birth to a daughter named Ani. They both were born in a rented house. Three years after she conceived again and gave birth to a fourth child, a son named Sudung. Two years later she conceives and gave birth to a fifth child, a son named Giat. Two years later mom conceives again and gave birth to twin son and daughter named Anes and Anna. Then my father has seven children, one his firstborn girl was born in his country Pansurnapitu and the other six children was born in Jakarta. And so this is the account of Karmel's children that line of them meet the date of the birthday: August, Ani, Giat, and the mixed-twin: Anes, a son, and Anna, a daughter. Sudung and Theo were something like twin for they were born in the same month; Sudung, the fourth son was born on 1st-12 and Theo the firstborn daughter, was the last of the annual celebrated birthday of the family, 12th-12.

In year 1972, a pastor was asked Karmel to be an elder in a church near his house. He refused it and prefers to lead men's choir ministry. Dad had refused the calling for about two years. In the other occasion, mom was called by her relatives in her country that her mother, grandma, was hard sick and dying. Therefore she went there taken care her in her last days. In the midst of that time, dad was suffering serious illness, infection on his eye. Therefore he cannot come to the church and lead the men choir. The pastor, who later became Arch Bishop, visited him and prophesying that he suffered this due to he rejected the office of an elder. Then dad replied him that he will receive it soon after mom got back. Then he inaugurated to be an elder in year 1974, and his name became Sintua (the elder) KP Panggabean (Gen. 12: 4-6 and 7-8).

The surrounding situation was cruel where they fighting each other to capture the land. Even the thief was in action to steal the precious things from our house. Then someone comes and gave dad a brochure of new housing in Depok 2, outside Jakarta. Dad gives it to mom and ask her agree to move. But mom was rejected. Dad asked her: "why?" She replied: **"you are an elder, you cannot live the calling. And look at your children here: you are the only son of your father. But now you have seven children. Don't forget the God's mercy upon you".** Then dad answered her and promises that **he would not live the calling**. But mom asks **how come for there is no church probably near the new house.** And thus dad replied that **he will found a church there and gathered the people.** But again mom asked him **how you found the people to found a church and how to build it. Dad answered her and believed that could be fifty people of our ethnical people live in the new housing and he can use our house for the church before he found a land for the Church.** For this answer, mom was finally agreed to move. For he has appointed to be a financial administrator, dad have to come back to Pulomas Jakarta before he resign from the Church.

On the first occasion on his first visit to buy the house he try to find the information from the local government if there is a Batak church near the house. But unfortunately the local government told that there is no a Batak ethnical church near the house. And the government was only provided a land for ecumenical church for all Protestant denomination in Samiaji street and a land for Catholic Church in Sadewa street. To know this situation dad was up-set for now he would leave the ministry as an elder. But he then ask the local government to give him the list of our ethnical people who had already buy the new houses around our home, where the list was include Moslem people, Adventist, Catholic, and Pentacostal denomination. The local government with his staff Saribu promised to give him the list at the day dad gets the key of the door. Dad was then went back to our home with joy because of the list and told mom that there are fifty people in the new housing. With this list then dad visit them door to door asked them whether they are Christian or not and whether they want to found a Batak ethnical church. Then Dad came back again in the other day to get the key and also the list of Batakness. Dad was also bought a land near our house and plant vegetable. In the visitation, dad was accompanied by his friend Sormean. He lives near our house. At first, they found only five families who agree to found the church and meet for the first time to prepare for the Sunday meeting. The other reject the invitation due to in their opinion St KP Panggabean had no land to build the Church, while the government only provides the land for Oikumene. Therefore they replied: tu Oikumene do hami, that they had decided to be member of Oikumene. This is includes St Kendari and Younger. Latter when the government gave the land for Batak Church, they were included in the first generation of the member and elder of Batak Church in Depok 2. Dad ask the local Bishop to permit them to found a church within the Congregation. The local Bishop advises that we have the permit to found the church in the Congregation as long as we can found the ministry including the woman ministry, the youth and Sunday school. Then they found the woman ministry leaded by Mrs Ruslan, mom, and asks Theo, the firstborn daughter to be a Sunday school teacher (three years later she resign from Sunday school teacher) and found youth ministry. Then they decided to have the first Sunday meeting at 14 October 1979 at the house of St. KP Panggabean. The first pastor to preach is Rev Tuan, a student of dad in his country, and St. KP Panggabean to be the elder to lead the worship and liturgy. And in the next month they decide to elect some of the first family member added to be an elder. This first elder graduation is included St. Sormean and they choose St. KP Panggabean as a Guru Huria (the head of the Church). The Church growing and the member is increasing in the coming years. For this reason, therefore they asked the local government permits to use school for the Sunday worship. This was happened for about three months after the foundation of the Church. The Church for temporary was to be subordinate to the greatest church in Jakarta at Sudirman. And Batak Church in Depok 2 is subordinate to Batak Church in Depok 1 in the year 1980 after the Bishop comes to bless the church as symbolical to the birth of the church.

Then comes the times when the union ecumenical church that has been initiated by the local government failed to unity and decided to separate and found their own denomination. The ecumenical church failed to start the erection to build the Church for the member is lowest government employee and they were prefer to refurnish their own new house. For this reason the local government decided to give the land to those who able to built the house of the Lord and ask all the denomination to meet. In the meeting the local government asked West Indonesia protestant church as they the biggest in the member, to be the first denomination asked whether they ready to build the house of the Lord. But they replied that they will build outside the new housing. Therefore the local government went to the Batak Church as the second biggest in the member. The local government asks: "Do the Batak Church have ability to build the house of the Lord?" **St. KP Panggabean answered the local government with a palm hand: "I am ready and able to build the house of the Lord."** Then the local government fall the hammer three times decides that the land given to Batak Church in Depok 2 for free and the official certificate of the land received by St. KP Panggabean. Now St. KP Panggabean has twelve the Promised Land consists of eight land inheritance of his father and four lands that God gives to him includes: home, one land for plantation, and the land for the Church and the land of aunt. Therefore he has to keep twelve of the Promised Land for his heritance such as the twelve Lands for the twelve tribes of Israel. One day after the Land was taken over, at the morning dad asks permission to his wife to visit the land. Mom advises dad to go with his son the fourth child, Sudung, to visit the land as his heir. At there the fourth child asks his father what this land for? Is this for the house or plantation? No, St. KP Panggabean answered no, it is for the Church. In other occasion in the next visit, St. KP Panggabean asks the fourth child accompanied by the fifth son Giat and the sixth son Anes. The elders then were elected the committee to collect money from the government, and the Richest and they had an event to collect money for building and the accessories such as live drama where the firstborn daughter as the main actress and St Rumah as the director and transcriptor. The building starts in erection. For the first development the building was only build the pillars only and the roof, without wall and floor. The development of the building takes time and money, therefore it developed gradually. And day by day the member of the church is growth in numbers. Then the elder decide to add the member of the elders. This is includes Tolut. He has persuaded St Sormean to ask dad so that he was elected in addition as the new elders. Tolut knows that St Sormean is the closest friend of St. KP Panggabean. Whatever dad told to St Sormean, he would agree, in turn whatever St Sormean thought, dad would agree as well. On the year 1985 St Sormean breath his last and death.

In the midst of his calling, on year 1980 St. KP Panggabean also found the union of Panggabean family in Depok. This is the first union of Panggabean in Jakarta. Therefore when the organization of Panggabean in Jakarta founded, union Panggabean of Depok did not need to inaugurate by the committee because they are already founded. This union is a fellowship of love so that family member of Panggabean was taking care and love each other share their burden and blessings according to the Bible. The gathering was using Bible for preaching, sing the hymnal and praying. The union also is the committee when one of the members had a family wedding, sickness and funeral etc. While St. KP Panggabean obeyed God's calling, he also worked as private teacher, therefore his relative called him Guru or teacher. He must work in various schools to meet his family needs. Sometimes the fourth son asked by mom to bring dad food in a school. When rain comes down, mom was also asked the fourth son to pick up dad with an umbrella so he cannot wet. In the beginning of the Church, sometimes the fourth son was assigned to send an invitation to the member so that they were not forgot about the schedule and place of the event. Even when the fourth son was 8 years old, mom was always took him to accompanied her to meet woman fellowship in Depok Timur for she always forget her friends' house. And Mom also ever assigned the fourth son to bring coffee to the elders whenever there is no office boy. St KP Panggabean was initiated also to found Batak tribes union around his house and elected to be the head of the committee. They were bound and happy in the union. When St KP Panggabean was in turn to be the host of the gathering, all people would come. They were respected him and feel the union was worth for them

(Gen. 12:2). When St Sitor's house was burned by fire, St KP Panggabean was asked the union to help.

CHAPTER THREE

The Quarreling Of Abram And Lot; Pulomas Setting

His sister, Aunt Ready had married in 1963 with Sihol. He likes to be called by his friend with **Lot**uk (means: abscess in head). **Lot**uk and his family were known about their bad habit in Pansurnapitu. Therefore St. KP Panggabean not allowed their relationship and said that he would not come to their wedding in Pansurnapitu. But mom pleases him that he should come to his only sister. They move also to Jakarta and live in Pulomas next to the house of St. KP Panggabean. Dad who was the chief of the community named the street at front of his house with Pelita, to copy PELITA's Nation-Development Plan by President Soeharto, and aunt Ready house with the Church or Gereja for there is Batak Church in Pulomas. Then they move to that house. But then comes to the event when we know that **Lot**uk was having an affair relationship with other woman and sent away her from his house. Aunt came to our house, wipe and told that she has been sent away by **Lot**uk. Dad advises her not move from the house and promises that he will take him to the court. Then dad with a help of his relative take him to the court and reported to the Judge that **Lot**uk was having an affair and sent her wife away. At January 24, 1979 the court decided that the land included the house will be aunt possession and they have to separate. When this happened, the only son of aunt was dead. **Lot**uk was acts like Lot which in the first persuade aunt Ready to be his wife and to be relative of St. KP Panggabean. After **Lot**uk became rich and established, for he had been relative of St. KP Panggabean and blessed by God, He act like Lot who commit coup to send his wife away. After the separation, Dad assigned the second son as the oldest son to accompanied aunt and aunt pay school for him. Now there are twelve Lands that were St. KP Panggabean possession, include the house of aunt. Dad also assigned the fourth son as the second the oldest son to accompany the fourth son in aunt house Pulomas whenever holiday. Even when aunt went to outside Jakarta to go to Yogyakarta for vacation and visit her parents, our grandparents, in our country, the fourth son was assigned by dad to accompany her. But when aunt remarried with Sitor, we went back to our father house. One day **Lot**uk re-married again with a woman from Java and plan to make her to be boru panggabean. St. KP Panggabean told disagreement and told how **Lot**uk hurt his family and also Aunt Ready at Family union. But they refused to feel the same hurt of Guru St. KP Panggabean and aunt Ready. A couple years latter **Lot**uk's wife dead and at the funeral **Lot**uk suddenly dead as well and buried in the same hole.

One of **Lot**uk's daughter cannot accept the struggle of poverty she has and then she burn herself.

CHAPTER FOUR

The Coup d' Ecclesia (The Quarreling Of Abraham's herdsmen and Lot's herdsmen); Samiaji Street Setting

Ge 13:1 So Abram went up from Egypt to the Negev, with his wife and everything he had, and Lot went with him. Abram had become very wealthy in livestock and in silver and gold. From the Negev he went from place to place until he came to **Bethel**, to the place between Bethel and Ai where his tent had been earlier and where **he had first built an altar. There Abram called on the name of the LORD.** Now Lot, who was moving about with Abram, also had flocks and herds and tents. But the land could not support them while they stayed together, for their possessions were so great that they were not able to stay together. And quarreling arose between Abram's herdsmen and the herdsmen of Lot. **So Abram said to Lot, "Let's not have any quarreling between you and me, or between your herdsmen and mine**, for **we are brothers**. Is not the whole land before you? Let's part company. If you go to the left, I'll go to the right; if you go to the right, I'll go to the left." Lot looked up and saw that the whole plain of the Jordan was well watered, like the garden of the LORD, like the land of Egypt, toward Zoar. (This was before the LORD destroyed Sodom and Gomorrah.) So Lot chose for himself the whole plain of the Jordan and set out toward the east. **The two men parted company: Abram lived in the land of Canaan**, while **Lot lived among the cities of the plain and pitched his tents near Sodom.**

Tolut was come from the same country of mom. He could be said is our mom's relatives. We called it Tulang rorobot or uncle of mother's line. And He called mom aunt. His forefather was brother with forefather of grandma. Around year 1980-1982, when Christmas come the firstborn daughter was try her skillful to make a cake. Mom was asked her to make a cake for Tolut as uncle in law relationship. For this, Tolut come to House and bring candy to our house at New Year. Tolut's wife was so glamourous. She doesn't look to her husband which is only a lowest state employee. She bought a very expensive dress using collected money of the church when Tolut was in office of church finance. Then Tolut came to our house bow down to mom legs and cry for his wife iniquity. He persuaded dad to keep this secret and promised to change with the same amount. Then comes the time when dad feel that he was unable to continue his job both as a private teacher and Guru Huria (the head of the Church) at the same time. Therefore he asks the pastor, Rev. Condor permission to resign as the office of Guru Huria. At the time he asked, the pastor was rejected. The pastor was come from the same country of mom and Tolut. His father was an elder in his country and also Tolut's father. They both quarelling for Tolut's father shop was opened when Sunday meeting and Tolut's father was a corrupt when he was in office of church finance. When Rev. Condor was assigned by the Arch Bishop to hold the office of Batak Church in Depok 1, Tolut was refused to receive him for their family quarelling background history. Then come one day at the meeting of the elders, the letter of resign from dad was read again in the meeting and all the members that persuaded by Tolut agree to elect Tolut to replace. Dad was not known that this meeting was already prepared by all the elder members to coup de 'ecclesia dad leaded by Tolut. They have a number of meetings in their house for this. After the meeting, dad went back home and told the event to his wife. They both were shocking. The fourth son actually woke-up and heard when dad told this event to mom in his bed. This was the third test of his calling and makes him and mom in grief. The firstborn daughter advises dad to move to other Protestant Church for this fate. But dad told her boldly, **"Daong inang, hubordit do na paet I; no dear I will eat this bad medicine".** Then St. KP Panggabean and Mom and St Rumah report this event to local Bishop. St Rumah said that Tolut actually persuaded him to be his group but he refused it. Local Bishop understands of what St. KP Panggabean suffering. He advises St. KP Panggabean not to leave his calling as sintua and also Mom to stay involve in women ministry. He promises to change Rev. Condor with Rev. Erikson.

And Rev. Erikson assigned to repair the ministry. As the punishment, there is no hand over the office from Rev. Condor to Rev. Erikson. But Tolut succeed to persuade Rev. Erikson to be his group. And Tolut remains to be Guru Huria for more than 20 years even though the pastor comes and go to our church. He was persuaded the pastor and most of the elders to be his group so that he could maintain his position even it was elected by vote for more than three times each five years period. In year 2000, when Rev. Turun was the leader of the Batak Church in Depok 1, there was an election for the office of Guru Huria, the leader of the Batak Church in Depok 2. Rev. Turun had already known that St KP Panggabean was the founder of the Church. He was asked St. KP Panggabean to elected back to be Guru Huria until he get pension due to his age is 65 years old. St. KP Panggabean agreed to held the office of Guru Huria until pension. But when Rev Ateng was the pastor of Depok 1 to replace Rev. Turun, Tolut was again get back to be elected the office of Guru Huria. At the end of his ministry, dad celebrated it in the church. Church gave him gold pin named Batak Church in Depok 2 and mom got golden ring. St Kendari cries at the event and said that he ever want to hit St. KP Panggabean by his car for Tolut had persuade him to hate St. KP Panggabean. Rev. Ateng invites dad St. KP Panggabean and all the elders to meet to talk about the history of the church and the quarelling. At that time, the fourth son actually wants to accompany his dad for he was worried about his father security. Mom asked dad what you want to talk to them and advised dad to talk boldly. At the meeting Tolut was denied that dad St. KP Panggabean was the founder of the Batak church in Depok 2 and denied that he was received the land from the government. But dad told him boldly that he doesn't matter with this. Rev Ateng then promoted to Bandung and replaced by Rev Roma. And for Depok 2, Tolut and their friends were asked to add Rev Kali as assistant pastor. But Rev. Kali was not good in preaching at the pulpit. Therefore they ask the Local Bishop to provide another pastor. Thus Local Bishop assigns Rev Simson to be assistant pastor in Depok 2 in 2005. On the first time, Tolut was trying to persuade and invite him to eat in a restaurant and talks. But Rev Simson was rejected the invitation. The invitation was initiation so that Rev Simson agreed as subordinate of Tolut and he could maintain his position. Then the letter came from Arch Bishop appointed Rev Simson to be the leader of the Church as per the new regulation. But the local Bishop sent the letter of appointment to Tolut, and he kept it secretly. The Arch Bishop and local Bishop was support Tolut for they need his vote for the election of Arch Bishop in the General Synod. This was makes all the people raise in anger. Shortly, the elder makes vote to choose who is the leader of the Church, Uluan ni Huria, whether Tolut or Rev Simson. At that time the elder meeting was find no agreement. Then comes the fifth son to the elder room, Consistory, where the elders met with Rev. Roma and warned him not to make riot in the church that found by his dad. He was inspired by the discussion between

Dad, mom and the fourth son, a day before. He hears it secretly and hides in his room. St Sitor was thanks to the fifth son effort. This was an ice breaking so that Tolut's group were frightening and fear. St Sitor said that the fifth son talk was boldly but makes them fear. Mom said they did not know and ask him to do it. The fourth son at that time advised the fifth son not to involve too much. But later he understood what the fifth son did was to protect his father and therefore he get the firstborn blessing also. Dad also had warned Rev Roma in the local meeting. But Rev Roma's wife was deny dad. A couple month after this his wife dead. Finally the elders elected Rev Simson as the new leader of the Church. Then he assigns a committee to audit the finance of the church. Finally the committee found a corruption in the finance report when Tolut was the leader of the Church. Then Rev Simson as the leader of the Church told mom to make a list of the member of the church to ask the leader of the church to makes a vote to decide whether Tolut punished by Ruhut Parmahanion dohot Paminsangon or excommunicates as the elder. Mom organized to collect signs from the church member and Dad was the first person to sign the list. Because according to St Sitor, it should be dad the first person to sign the list and then the others will dare to continue. Finally most of the elders agree that Tolut excommunicated because most of the member of the Church agree to excommunicate him. The firstborn daughter said to his father, you were blessed to see the fall of Tolut in your old age. Latter the Local Bishop permit him to found a church in Kota and he became Guru Huria. He found a church and subordinate to the other church. But he and his elders colleague continue corrupted. And he destroyed the official certificate of the land that had been given before by St. KP Panggabean.

Tolut and his herdsmen thought the Land is their own, for they have occupied the Land and get benefit from it. In 1994 the youth named him with abbreviation his family name **Lbt**. He acted like **Lot** who at first persuade Abraham to accompany him to the Promised Land but later when he grown up, he commit coup. He thought the land is his own now. He became rich but Abraham become old, and has no child. Lot thought he would not become heresy for he had learned the religion from Abraham and he had been prosper, give lot of the sacrifices for God and had been serve God as his servant. Lot did not know that there is personal God's promise blessing and curse between God and Abraham; for those who blessed and cursed Abraham and his descendants. And God would angry against someone who curses the descendants of Abraham (Gen. 31:24). Tolut thought that they had been put their properties there and Church have been refurnished with granite, therefore the Church was now become their own. Mom told that before, they were The Poor. But after they had stay and pray in the Promised Land, they were become richest with beautiful and smart babies. They even did not buy any money to rent the Land. They had revolt and occupy the Land for over 20 years. They thought the church now becomes their own. They even did not thank for my dad effort in the past, and they did not accept that God had given the Promised Land to St. KP Panggabean where they stay and pray there. They don't realize and even did not read the Bible and even cannot believe that the Land was already given to St. KP Panggabean. And they did not understand that Lot who wants to coup Abraham was cursed by God (Gen. 19:26f and 30-38ff). They don't realize or even they were entered by the evil to mocking, laughing and hate the servant of God. They don't even accept that the Land is the Promised Land and had been given to St. KP Panggabean and his descendants as the covenant fellowship with the Almighty God. When Tolut was in office of the Head of the Church or Guru Huria, there were happened the dead of men's choir ministry, and youth ministry. Even the Sunday meeting was attended by a few people only. But women choir ministry, Sunday School, and trumpet musician were still active in ministry due to there are St. KP Panggabean's family in the ministry. Mom involved in Women ministry, Sudung, Giat and Anes in Sunday School, and August in trumpet. The fourth son had also found three times Tolut preach in the pulpit was far away from the biblical context that he read, even he was not discussed one of its verse. Tolut thought that the passage is not important, and he more cares with his own idea. Tolut also had preached that the youth should not diligent to study the Bible and the Sunday School teacher is not a servant of God. Then there is a debate in the final judgment. God asks Lot and their descendant, the unbelievers who comes to the Heaven: "who are you; where are you come from?" They replied: "I am your people, God. I am the relative of Father Abraham. We have been worshiping you in our Church and live in our Land for a long time". But God replied them: "I don't know you. Where is your certificate of the Land? I didn't give the Land for you. I had given the Land for Abraham, his wife Sarah and his descendants Isaac, Jacob and the twelve tribes of Israel". But Lot argues: "But I have been a couple years serve you as the elder". God denied him: "I have no call you to be my people and to be my servant. You are a persuade servant. I have only called Abraham, his wife Sarah, his descendants Isaac, Jacob and the twelve tribes of Israel. In fact, I don't recognize you all, Go away !" Later Rev. Atcng failed in his ministry in Bandung Church and Rev. Roma found corrupted as well in Depok 1 Church and he had quarrelling with the elders. A couple of month later Rev. Condor, Rev. Ateng and Rev. Roma's wife were dead when dad and mom were health. The church member spoke this event with: Marmatean halaki, means: They dead gradually one by one while dad and mom still comes to the Church. Dad and mom come to visit at Rev. Condor and Rev. Ateng funeral. The firstborn daughter advised dad to visit them even dad was walk by his stick. Then Tolut's herdsmen includes: Si Deang, and Ramot had punished as well to ex-communicate. A Batak pastor preached in the pulpit: in eighties most of the students who applied Seminary were proudly testified that they were called to be pastor. But begin in nineties until present, most of them said that they were became pastor for it would be easy to find the job even they have to suffer assigned in a remote area. A few of them was remains testifies that they were called. But the question is: who calls them? That is why now we have quarreling in the church; for most of them were persuaded pastors and elders.

CHAPTER FIVE

The Quarreling Of Abraham and Lot; Pansurnapitu Setting

G randdad St Cyrus Panggabean has eight of land consist of paddy fields, land for vegetables and to keep his pig and land for his three houses and the jungle of myrrh trees. The paddy field that his own was claimed by his cousin, Berani, his older brother from different mother. The claimer was asked his brother, Ingot's father, cousin of our relative from granddad, to occupy the Land. Then granddad went to the court to ask government to execute. This news was told to his son St. KP Panggabean. Then he went to his father house and told his father to cancel the complaint to the court and let the relatives takes the land as long as he lives. St. KP Panggabean was advises that because the relatives was has no other jobs and he has no child anymore. His cousin, Ingot's father, our relative from father of granddad even suggest dad to take granddad from Pansurnapitu to Jakarta and buried in Jakarta, He advised this in order that he could occupy the land. A couple months after dad canceled from the court, he and his brother breath his last and death, when granddad still have a long live. In year 2000, the fourth son asked dad to asked government to certify the land. Dad went there accompanied by mom, aunt Ready, the second son and the fifth son.

In the other occasion, Ingot's father, our relative from father of granddad, our cousin from three generation above us was claim the land beside the house who are the land for vegetable and to keep a pig. He even asked granddad to go with his son to Jakarta so that he could occupy the Land. But St. KP Panggabean was so generous. He has a heart like Abraham, full of compassion. He has let his house to be the venue of the marriage of his daughter, Tari. Even, dad was helped her to fulfill her need to be a nurse in a hospital. One of his son, Ingot, was already went to Jakarta as well to find a job. He always comes to our home in Depok to asked dad to help him to find a job. Then dad taken him to his friend and asked for job. They get it. Then dad was asked by him to prepare his married. In hearing this, the granddad was angry to dad and asked did you know how they treat me? Why you so generous to him? Dad argued the problem in the village let be locally; it is better not inheritance to their descendant. Even when the New Year's eve comes, he went to our house in Depok to pray in the New Year's eve with us. When St Cyrus was dead and the claimer was dead as well, Ingot was influenced by his mother and their brothers to fight against dad. Ingot acts like Lot, who at first in his young ask Abraham to go with him. But after he established and independent now he wants to coup Abraham. In year 2000 when dad and aunt were planned to certify the Land by the government, they were angry and put also some false witnesses. They were discussed in one house, and they said that the land is for housing; means that the land is belongs to them also. Therefore they have the same right to use the land. Aunt Ready asked to Ingot's family: why do I never hear the term that the land is for housing whenever my father lives? Why now changed? Dad was generous to give him the land but in turn we were not a related family anymore. St. KP Panggabean thus excommunicates Ingot and his family as his relative. He said we have to parted company (Gen.13:9-11). Ingot name mean remember, but he forget the Dad' generous in helping him and his family. Ingot's brother, Tolouse, found a foundation of a house at the land to say that they were the owner of the land. To realized this fact, the fourth son was advises dad to ask government certified for all the Land in the granddad house. In year 2008, Mom also went to Pansurnapitu to continue to certify the paddy field lands accompanied by the second son and the expenses was provided by the fourth son. Now almost the land has its certification with an exception: the house and the jungle of myrrh trees, Horsik. One day, when St KP Panggabean visited his parents, one of village people who uneducated told him that the water well beside his father house was not his father's own for it was built by Government (Gen.21:25, 30; 26:20). He called the well is 'sumur PELITA'. But St KP Panggabean argued him that it was not built by Government; but one day there was thick rain and storm and thunder and suddently water comes out besides his father house. St KP Panggabean wonders to him why he doesn't ashamed who was not graduated from primary school, teaches him about government project.

CHAPTER SIX

Hagar And Ishmael Sent Away

Ge 16:1 Now Sarai, Abram's wife, **had borne him no children.** But she had an Egyptian maidservant named Hagar; *Ge 16:2* so she said to Abram, "The LORD has kept me from having children. Go, sleep with my maidservant; perhaps I can build a family through her." Abram agreed to what Sarai said. *Ge 16:3* So after Abram had been living in Canaan ten years, Sarai his wife took her Egyptian maidservant Hagar and gave her to her husband to be his wife. *Ge 16:4* He slept with Hagar, and she conceived. When she knew she was pregnant, **she began to despise her mistress**. *Ge 21:8* The child grew and was weaned, and on the day Isaac was weaned Abraham held a great feast. *Ge 21:9* But Sarah saw that the son whom Hagar the Egyptian had borne to Abraham was mocking, *Ge 21:10* and she said to Abraham, "Get rid of that slave woman and her son, for that slave woman's son will never share in the inheritance with my son Isaac." *Ge 21:11* The matter distressed Abraham greatly because it concerned his son. *Ge 21:12* But God said to him, "Do not be so distressed about the boy and your maidservant. Listen to whatever Sarah tells you, because it is through Isaac that your offspring will be reckoned. *Ge 21:13* I will make the son of the maidservant into a nation also, because he is your offspring." *Ge 21:14* Early the next morning Abraham took some food and a skin of water and gave them to Hagar. He set them on her shoulders and then sent her off with the boy.

Keturah, Medan and Midian Sent Away

Ge 25:1 Abraham took another wife, whose name was Keturah. *Ge 25:2* She bore him Zimran, **Jokshan**, **Medan, Midian**, Ishbak and Shuah. *Ge 25:3* Jokshan was the father of Sheba and Dedan; the descendants of Dedan were the Asshurites, the Letushites and the Leummites. *Ge 25:4* The sons of Midian were Ephah, Epher, Hanoch, Abida and Eldaah. All these were descendants of Keturah. *Ge 25:5* Abraham left everything he owned to Isaac. *Ge 25:6* But while he was still living, **he gave gifts to the sons of his concubines and sent them away from his son Isaac to the land of the east.**

When dad was in charge as Guru Huria, church leader, there is a gossip blow from a woman that said dad was corrupted and stolen money. She hates dad and her face show that she hates dad very much. She wrote a letter to him. This letter was kept by mom and read it repeatedly for several times. Because of this, mom was drops of depression and suffers brain sickness and for several times sent to the hospital. Doctor found the source of her sickness was from Church issue and he advised to destroy the letter. But one day the church found that her husband was corrupted. Then their family went away without permission from the church.

One woman, a wife of the member of the elders, was hate dad and talks loud before him. When dad wants to ask her husband's sign as the secretary of the church, he asks the fourth child to her house. At the other occasion, he assigns the fourth son and fifth son to ask signing a letter. Latter this woman dead in her young age, while Dad and mom has a long live. The other woman who has her ambition to be a conductor of the woman choir, was hated mom due to mom's skill was better than her, even they both get the same training. Sometime later she had serious illness and cannot attend to the church and lying weak in her bed for several years. One day the woman ministry visiting her including mom. She cries when she saw mom was health. Later she died, while mom and dad had a long live. She thought she could coup d' ecclesia St. KP Panggabean's wife and occupy the land.

In the first years of Batak Church in Depok 2, the firstborn daughter was asked by dad to be the first Sunday school teacher. After three years, the firstborn daughter was asked to resign for she want to work. In year 1994, in the reign of Tolut, the fourth son was volunteered to join the Sunday school teacher for there are no male teacher. But when Tolut banned the teenager service, all of Sunday school teacher, which they both were the same committee decides to resign as well. Then the fifth son and the sixth son were called to replace by their own initiative to be Sunday school teacher for about two years. The second son was called to be musical in church, both trumpet and organist. The third child and the seventh child, both are girls, prefer to serve their dad and mom, to take care the household, the kitchen and the food.

In the reign of Tolut as Guru Huria, the fourth son was tries to joining the teenager service and Sunday school. At first it is good. But latter there is a girl who have been joining the service before him becoming mocking to him. Even she angry and hate to the fourth son. Her mother was converted from Ismaelite. In fact the fourth child was not skillful than her. But at the biblical exegesis, the son of St. KP Panggabean was better than theirs. One day when the fourth child had told that the Church land was his father's own, the girl was laughing. Even she is laughing when she saw dad was fault to read the liturgy in the Church. At that time, the fourth son was angry upon her and she asked forgiveness. But when she saw the fourth son was late in find his mate, she laughs when met him. The girl is like Hagar and Ishmael who came from pagan, then they excommunicate back to Pagan including their descendants. The fourth son cannot understand about this in the past. But after the dead of his father, and mom prophesying that our family is like Israel for several times, he has sureness that the story of the Bible is fulfilled in the family. A series of repeated struggle and the same suffering of the Israelites, the holy war between the descendants of Abraham versus the descendants of Hagar, Ishmael; and the descendants of Lot; i.e: Moab and Ammon; and descendants of Keturah: sons of Medan, Midian, Ephah, Asshurites; and descendants of Esau; i.e: Herod, Amalekites. The fourth son believes that those descendants of Ishmael are inter-married with the descendants of Lot, Hagar and Ishmael, Keturah and Esau. And they were the eternal enemy of Israel until present.

One old woman who proudly called as the anak Medan (Son of Medan city in North Sumatera province) who was poor, later her sons became prosper and had many children. She became boastful and despised the sons and daughters of St. KP Panggabean. She and her daughter mocking, hate and despise them. For she now could give church more than anyone. When the Church celebrated their annual birthday, she always dances with her favorite song: "Si anak Medan" and gave the money to the Church. They are like Hagar and Ishmael who were mocking Sarah and Isaac. And then there is a debate in the final judgment. God asks Hagar, Ishmael and their descendant, the unbelievers who comes to the Heaven: "who are you; where are you come from?" They said: "We are your people, God. We belong to our great great Father Abraham. We have been worshiping you in our Church and live in our Land for a long time". But God replied them: "I don't know you. Where is your certificate of the Land? I didn't give the Land for you. I had given the Land for Abraham, his wife Sarah and his descendants Isaac, Jacob and the twelve tribes of Israel". Hagar and Ishmael argue: "But I have been a couple of years serve you as the elder". God replied to them: "I have no called you to be my people and my servant; I have only called Abraham, his wife Sarah, and his descendants: Isaac, Jacob and the twelve tribes of Israel. Truly I don't recognize you all, Go away!" Then comes Keturah, Medan and Midian and their descendants to the Heaven. God asks them: "Who are you; where are you come from?" They said: "We are your people, God. We belong to our great great Father Abraham. We have been worshiping you in our Church and live in our Land for a long time". But God replied them: "I don't know you. Where is your certificate of the Land? I didn't give the Land for you. I had given the Land for Abraham, his wife Sarah and his descendants Isaac, Jacob and the twelve tribes of Israel". But they argue: "We have been gave you a lot of sacrifices from our prosperities for we are richest". But God said them: "I have no call you to be my people, and my servant; I have only called Abraham, his wife Sarah, and his descendants: Isaac, Jacob and the twelve tribes of Israel. You became rich for you live in Abraham's land. And God asked Abraham: "Do you know them all?" Abraham said: "Yes, but they are not my descendants. I have already excommunicate them". Then God sent them away: "You all, Go!"

CHAPTER SEVEN

The Family Burial Site Of Abraham

Ge 23:1 Sarah lived to be a hundred and twenty-seven years old. *Ge 23:2* She died at Kiriath Arba (that is, Hebron) in the land of Canaan, and Abraham went to mourn for Sarah and to weep over her. *Ge 23:3* Then Abraham rose from beside his dead wife and spoke to the Hittites. He said, *Ge 23:4* "I am an alien and a stranger among you. Sell me some property for a burial site here so I can bury my dead." *Ge 23:5* The Hittites replied to Abraham, *Ge 23:6* "Sir, listen to us. You are a mighty prince among us. Bury your dead in the choicest of our tombs. None of us will refuse you his tomb for burying your dead." *Ge 23:7* Then Abraham rose and bowed down before the people of the land, the Hittites. *Ge 23:8* He said to them, "If you are willing to let me bury my dead, then listen to me and intercede with Ephron son of Zohar on my behalf *Ge 23:9* so he will sell me the cave of Machpelah, which belongs to him and is at the end of his field. Ask him to sell it to me for the full price as a burial site among you." *Ge 23:10* Ephron the Hittite was sitting among his people and he replied to Abraham in the hearing of all the Hittites who had come to the gate of his city. *Ge 23:11* "No, my lord," he

41

said. "Listen to me; I give you the field, and I give you the cave that is in it. I give it to you in the presence of my people. Bury your dead." *Ge 23:12* Again Abraham bowed down before the people of the land *Ge 23:13* and he said to Ephron in their hearing, "Listen to me, if you will. I will pay the price of the field. Accept it from me so I can bury my dead there." *Ge 23:14* Ephron answered Abraham, *Ge 23:15* "Listen to me, my lord; the land is worth four hundred shekels of silver, but what is that between me and you? Bury your dead." *Ge 23:16* Abraham agreed to Ephron's terms and weighed out for him the price he had named in the hearing of the Hittites: four hundred shekels of silver, according to the weight current among the merchants. *Ge 23:17* So Ephron's field in Machpelah near Mamre—both the field and the cave in it, and all the trees within the borders of the field—was deeded *Ge 23:18* to Abraham as his property in the presence of all the Hittites who had come to the gate of the city. *Ge 23:19* Afterward Abraham buried his wife Sarah in the cave in the field of Machpelah near Mamre (which is at Hebron) in the land of Canaan. *Ge 23:20* **So the field** and the cave **in it were deeded to Abraham** by the Hittites **as a burial site.**

When St. KP Panggabean was in charge as Guru Huria, at the Passover day, to commemorate the resurrection of Christ, the church was celebrate the event of the girls who come to the grave to anointing the body of Christ, with a service in the old grave that found in the time of Dutch government. The fourth son, even he was a Sunday school, was asked by dad to go there. Sometimes he met with Sunday school teacher there. When the service was ended, one of the grave committee told to St. KP Panggabean there is a man who buried there with same family name. He told that if the annual rent-grave is not pay by the family, the grave will sell to the others. In the other days, St. KP Panggabean was tries to find out the family line of the dead man. And finally he found that the dead man was his relative. Then he contacts the committee and bought the grave as his family burial site. In year 1992 granddad comes from Pansurnapitu to see grandma that had a treatment in Jakarta, but granddad illness was become worse and finally breath his last and death. Before St Cyrus has a dream met with the father of mom and he said greetings Horas. This was testified by mom. St. KP Panggabean was buried his father at his family burial site. Two years later her mother was death and buried beside his father. Before death, grandma has a dream that there are two visitors comes with white dress. After wake, grandma told mom. Grandma asked: Di jabunta do on? Is this our house? Yes, Mom replied. Grandma further said: Ai ro do dua halak marbaju na bontar. There are comes two visitors with white dress. Then mom advises her that grandma to deliver herself to God and ask forgiveness of her sins. His relatives Terima kasih help St KP Panggabean to ask the committee to let him buried his mother beside his father. St. KP Panggabean then buried his mother at his family burial site besides his father.

CHAPTER EIGHT

Jacob And Esau

Ge 25:19 This is the account of Abraham's son Isaac. Abraham became the father of Isaac, *Ge 25:20* and **Isaac was forty years old when he married Rebekah daughter of Bethuel the Aramean from Paddan Aram and sister of Laban the Aramean.** *Ge 25:21* **Isaac prayed to the LORD on behalf of his wife, because she was barren. The LORD answered his prayer, and his wife Rebekah became pregnant.** *Ge 25:22* The babies jostled each other within her, and she said, "Why is this happening to me?" So she went to inquire of the LORD. *Ge 25:23* **The LORD said to her, "Two nations are in your womb, and two peoples from within you will be separated; one people will be stronger than the other, and the older will serve the younger.** " *Ge 25:24* When the time came for her to give birth, there were twin boys in her womb. *Ge 25:25* **The first to come out was** red, and **his whole body was like a hairy** garment; so they named him Esau. *Ge 25:26* After this, his brother came out, with his hand grasping Esau's heel; so he was named Jacob. Isaac was sixty years old when Rebekah gave birth to them. *Ge 25:27* The boys grew up, and **Esau became a skillful** hunter, **a man of** the open country, while Jacob was a quiet man, staying among the tents. *Ge 25:28* Isaac, who had a taste for wild game, loved Esau, but Rebekah loved Jacob.

Ge 25:31 Jacob replied, "First **sell me your birthright.** *Ge 25:33* But Jacob said, "Swear to me first." **So he swore an oath to him, selling his birthright to Jacob.** *Ge 25:34* Then Jacob gave Esau some bread and some lentil stew. He ate and drank, and then got up and left. **So Esau despised his birthright.**

Ge 26:34 **When Esau was forty years old, he married Judith daughter of Beeri the Hittite, and also Basemath daughter of Elon the Hittite.** *Ge 26:35* **They were a source of grief to Isaac and Rebekah.**

Ro 9:6 It is not as though God's word had failed. **For not all who are descended from Israel are Israel.** *Ro 9:7* Nor because they are his descendants are they all Abraham's children. On the contrary, **"It is through Isaac that your offspring will be reckoned."** *Ro 9:8* In other words, it is not the natural children who are God's children, **but it is the children of the promise who are regarded as Abraham's offspring.** *Ro 9:9* For this was how the promise was stated: "At the appointed time I will return, and Sarah will have a son." *Ro 9:10* Not only that, but Rebekah's children had one and the same father, our father Isaac. *Ro 9:11* **Yet, before the twins were born or had done anything good or bad—in order that God's purpose in election might stand:** *Ro 9:12* **not by works but by him who calls—she was told, "The older will serve the younger."** *Ro 9:13* Just as it is written: **"Jacob I loved, but Esau I hated."**

Ge 37:3 Now **Israel loved Joseph more than any of his other sons**, because he had been born to him in his old age; and **he made a richly ornamented robe for him**. When his brothers saw that their father loved him more than any of them, **they hated him and could not speak a kind word to him**.

The fourth son was some kind like Jacob who was a quiet man, and likes to stay at home (Gen. 25:27). When he was on leave, he will go back to his father house. The fourth son was some kind like Joseph as well, for he helps his father to feed him, mom and all family when he got the work. He also works outside the Promised Land so that the family safe and secure in their needs (Gen.37:36; 50:20-21). Dad had given him a blue shirt batik Kalimantan which looks good when he was 19 years old. The firstborn daughter also had given him several times t-shirt which is a good one (Gen.37:3-4). To see this, the second son, and the fifth son and the sixth son were usually uses his shirts. This sometimes was makes him angry. Even the second son was like to use the trouser of the fourth son although it was too small for his waist. The children were always kidding their father that the fourth son was his favorite and mom also. But actually mom's favorite was the firstborn daughter. Mom always testifies that the firstborn daughter was generously helped her in family budget. So while Isaac love Esau and Rebekah love Jacob (Gen. 25:28) and Jacob love Joseph (Gen.37:3); St. KP Panggabean was love the fourth son and mom love the firstborn daughter. Later mom testifies that the wise of dad was come down to the fourth son. And the fourth son was contributes also to feed the family. By the way St. KP Panggabean was like Isaac who love to eat meat (Gen.25:28). Even this was contradicted to his healthy for he suffered hyper tension blood and heart attack. Therefore his children were kept the food away from his sight. In the gathering, his relatives testify and see that St. KP Panggabean and his wife, when they became old, their faces look like brother and sister (Gen. 12:13; 20:2; 26:7). In fact, our fore father, Panggabean and Hutabarat is brother in a family of Si Opat Pisoran, son of Guru Mangaloksa, in Batak Genealogy. When St. KP Panggabean was preaching in the ministry, he usually blesses the ministry with the words "may you bless with God the Lord (Gen.28:4)".

The fourth son and the firstborn daughter such as a twin because they both born in the same month December. The fourth son was born 1st-12 and the firstborn daughter 12th-12. The firstborn daughter was hairy at her hands and legs (Gen. 25:25), more than the others the children of St. KP Panggabean. The firstborn daughter is a beauty daughter and brilliant in her work (Gen. 25:27). Her career was developed from lowest staff as telephone operator then promoted into a junior staff and promoted again into Human resources Manager and finally she was promoted into General Manager, although she was only high school graduated. She is mom's favorite because after she get work she always help mom for the family issues especially money. After she graduated from high school, she asks dad to continue her study to college. But dad refused it because he cannot afford it. When the second son graduated from high school, dad asked to his sister, our aunt, to pay the college tuition. When the third child graduate from high school and asked to continue to college, dad again refuse the woman continue to the college because he cannot afford it. Then comes the fourth son graduate from high school, he asks to continue to university dad agree with him. Before dad was promise to sell the land near the house, that he buy after get a new house in Depok, for whom wants to continue the study to college. For this the firstborn daughter and the third child were jealous because dad only permits his sons to college but not his daughters (Gen.37:4, 11). Latter the seventh child studied at a college and the firstborn daughter pays the tuition and fees.

The firstborn daughter always gives the money to mom to help mom to fulfill all family needs and after she get promotion, she gave money as well to all the children of dad every month when she get the salary. The firstborn daughter was an excellent in his work. She gets promotion from low workers as telephone receptionist gradually into junior staff, senior staff, administration, finance staff, and human resources manager and finally promoted into highest position in the company as General Manager. Actually she said that she was asked by her boss to fill the Director position when the position was vacant. She has excellent skillful even though she was only graduated from high school (See Gen. 25:27). Her subordinate is the managers who graduated from university. And she likes travelling during holiday in open country. Then comes a day when a boy friend of her office persuaded her to be his wife. The man was pagan. But because he has not a son, he asks her to be his wife. Dad and mom did not agree with this relationship and asks the firstborn daughter to break up the relationship and not come late from the office. But she did not follow her dad command. They then married in Singapore. When she get pregnant, she came home and ask mom to prepare traditional cuisine golden fish from Batak named na ni arsik. Then she told that she was pregnant to her mother. But mom kept this for several times not to know dad. After mom told dad, dad become angry and plan to kill her (Gen 17:14), but mom pleasing him to reduce anger and give mercy on her for she has helped family. This was a source of grief to St. KP Panggabean and his wife (Gen.26:35). Even mom was fall down at the market when she bought fishes and vegetables. Then the firstborn daughter gives birth to a son and named him Heinze. The child was infected by tokso bacteria when he was born. And therefore he had a treatment for several times and the doctor advises to the firstborn daughter not bear the child anymore. When he was two years old he was late in communication, then their parents check him to the doctor and found that he was suffer hyperactive and need treatment for several years so that he can communicate, taught and reduce the effect of the bad attitude.

The life of the fourth son can be called there is no

big issue, while the other sons have their issue on hot temperature body which result weakness when their grown up. Mom always told that the fourth son is drinks milk more than the others and when he can eat, while the older brother and sisters with parents start meal he always wants to eat as well and said I have not addition meal before, I need now. Education for the fourth son was start from kindergarten school, while the older brother and sisters no. The school at new housing was not established yet. They have to use other school for temporary. There is no transportation at the new housing at that time. There is only private transportation but limited and occasionally. Therefore sometimes they have to walk through the river, paddy fields, and the plantation trees to get home. Therefore we complain to dad. This was told by the firstborn daughter in the future. For this, dad decide we move to Christian school were dad is the teacher at junior high school. In the future, the fourth son understand this historical event, that our complain is want to ask dad that we should have a school in Christian school, in your office so we could study the Bible, pray, and praise. At Christian school, the third child was started at fourth year. And the fourth son was started at second year. The first study at Christian school was to write the prayer Our heavenly Father and tested to profess on the next day. At the Christmas celebration, the school was given the Christmas gift by collecting money from student. The third child was got a story book children that was from the Bible of Luke. When the fourth son saw it, he asks to borrow to read it. Because he likes the book with pictures, he read it for several times. The fourth son was not realized about this at that time. Even he was amazed when in the Sunday school, his friends were cannot concentrate themselves to listen the teaching of teacher, while he was like and listen the story of the Bible. One day the teachers were having a test for all Sunday school students and the fourth son get the highest score among the other children. When he grown up, the fourth son was still cannot understand why he better than the others of his generation in studying the Bible. He even amazed why dad, the elder and ex-Guru Huria, was lack of homiletics on his preaching. Later the fourth son was find the answer that God graciously give him the talent because he was the son of St. KP Panggabean, the servant of God.

The main reason that dad did not bring us to that school for the tuition for private school was more expensive than government school. This was told by dad later as his salary is low with seven children. Therefore the fourth son was asked by him to get government high school. But the government school does not have a good Christian education. That is why when mom told us that in the past she had asked God to give her sons to continue family line and none of us follow her advises to be a pastor. After the fourth son graduate from high school, mom was asked him to study theological. But the fourth son was so weak and do not think that he should study theology. Dad to see the fourth son was so weak, allow him to take study engineering school. Before mom had asked the second child as her first son to study theology and be a pastor. But the second child was rejects it and prefer to choose music as his way of life. Dad was prophesying and said you cannot pay your meal by music. When the fourth son was teenager he was joined with the teenager service in the church. But when Tolut banned the ministry, he decided to continue to joint parachurch in Jakarta to found teenager and high school ministry in Depok. At that time, dad always angry with the fourth son that he went out from the Promised Land and involve in the other ministry. But the fourth son was not understands the angry of his dad. In 1996 when the fourth son had a visitation to a student house, he met with three pentacostal pastors. They were persuaded the fourth son to accept Spirit baptism and Immerse baptism. Even they mocking the fourth son for he told them that he was believe that he had already baptism and he didn't believe speak in tongue phenomena. The debate was so high in tension and then they asked the fourth son to pray and they were raised their hand to bless him. At night the fourth son feel something strange with his body. He feels unlike to bear his body on bed. He cannot sleep. Then he memorized the event in the morning. Therefore he prays to God to sent the spirit away from his body and asked God to help otherwise he will receive the faith of Pentacostal-Charismatic movement. He prays the same thing for three times and prays to God to curse them all. When he pray for the first time, he feels better. Then he decided to pray for the second time and he feels much better than before. Therefore he tries to pray the same thing for the third time. After he finished pray he fell to sleep. When he woke up he knew that God was besides him and he is God's favor.

CHAPTER NINE

Jacob Wrestles With God

Ge 32:24 **So Jacob was left alone, and a man wrestled with him** till daybreak. *Ge 32:25* When the man saw that he could not overpower him, **he touched the socket of Jacob's hip so that his hip was wrenched as he wrestled with the man.** *Ge 32:26* Then the man said, "Let me go, for it is daybreak." But Jacob replied, "I will not let you go unless **you bless me.**" *Ge 32:27* The man asked him, "What is your name?" "Jacob," he answered. *Ge 32:28* **Then the man said, "Your name will no longer be Jacob, but Israel,** because **you have struggled with God and with men and have overcome."** **and he was limping because of his hip.**

In year 2000, whenever the fourth son get job, he try to make a friend with a girl. But She rejected due to the fourth son was not independent. Then he tried to someone else. This time again was rejected by her mother. Even her mother was mocking St. KP Panggabean, Mom, the firstborn daughter, and the second son. If she knew all of St. KP Panggabean family, she would hate them all. Her mother was disgusting the family of St. KP Panggabean for they were poor. After broke up, the fourth son went to remote island to work in order to increase his wages and hope his finally find his mate on this small island. Six month after broke up, friend of the fourth son was contacting that she will be married. The fourth son became frustration and asked God why God let his servant mocked by woman such like Hagar and her son like Ishmael despised the servant of God descendants? Did he care? The fourth son was memorizing the suffering of his family to find their spouse. Start from the firstborn daughter then to the second son and the third child till the seventh child, we all suffer the same problem. The fourth son was asking God's blessing and remember to his father who is his servant. He compares to the member of the Church that has prosperity, and find their mates and give birth the children. They were mocking, laughing, and hate acting like Hagar and Ishmael and Keturah, Medan and Midian. The fourth son was heart break about a week and cannot find a way to pull this bad feeling. He even asks God to excommunicate that woman who acts like Hagar and Ishmael. Then when he wants to go to the office in the morning, he drives his motorcycle with full gear speed. When he feels are going to hit someone in front, he pushed the brake tightly but he can't and he hit the man but not hurt him. But the fourth son cannot stabilizing his motorcycle and fell down and broke his knee, right hand of his legs (Gen. 32:25, 31). Father of his friend was having an incident as well and broke his leg hit by other motor cycle. They bring him to traditional shaman for massage and get well back in a week. While the fourth son suffering three month in bed, and almost a year to recover. After a year, he went back to hospital to pull out the pin. The fourth son had been asked by his friends to have traditional massage as well, but he replied with a soft word to reject. And at that time the fourth son feels that he suffers like Jacob, but he is not sure. The pastor of the Church which he attended in Sunday service was visiting him twice. She asked the fourth children to be the leader of the youth. She testified as well to mom that the fourth son was a good man and diligently went to church. So when the fourth son was in the treatment, the family suffering famine again, for St. KP Panggabean was already pension.

Four months after that accident, the firstborn daughter had a huge temptation. She found corruption in her company involving from the lowest level into the Director. Therefore she was hate by the most of them and they try to found the way to sent away her from the company. They accused her back corrupted in a small amount finance report. But finally the owner found that they were corrupted. The Director and his group were sent away from the company. The Director asked shaman to attack the firstborn's heart. At night the firstborn was feel her heart so hard and feel she would died. She cried aloud and scream. Then the third child who accompanied her with the fifth son called the fourth son by phone. They were accompanied the firstborn daughter for there was an issue that her opposite, the Director was sent a pack and assign to kill her. The firstborn daughter asked the fourth son to keep her son whenever she died. But the fourth son asked her to pray to God. Then he pray for his sister for several times to ask God to deliver the temptation and remember the family of St KP Panggabean, his servant. When mom suddenly wake-up, the fourth son told this and advise her to pray as well. The third son and the fifth son cannot do anything unless crying. Then the third child asked the neighbor to bring the firstborn daughter to the hospital. The fourth son pray for several times to God to deliver his sister from the temptation though he was not knows what was happened. At the hospital, the firstborn daughter told this to Aunt Ready. Aunt Ready cries for the firstborn daughter suffering and wonder how a man like Director committed evil to her. The visitor of patient in the same room with the firstborn daughter was hear the story and come to close and ask to check with her spiritual ability. She said that the firstborn daughter was attacked by great evil to attack her heart. Then she asked the firstborn daughter permit to send the spirit away. After this event, the sixth son praises the fourth son who protected their sister (Gen. 49:8). Three months after this event, the third child suffer appendix inflammation and should treat immediate surgery in the hospital. The fourth son gives her the initial payment to register to the hospital and the fifth son accompanied her in the hospital.

CHAPTER TEN

God's Covenant With Abram

Ge 15:1 After this, the word of the LORD came to Abram in a vision: "Do not be afraid, Abram. I am your shield, your very great reward." But Abram said, "O Sovereign LORD, what can you give me **since I remain childless** and the one who will inherit my estate is Eliezer of Damascus?" **And Abram said, "You have given me no children; so a servant in my household will be my heir."** Then the word of the LORD came to him: **"This man will not be your heir, but a son coming from your own body will be your heir." He took him outside and said, "Look up at the heavens and count the stars—if indeed you can count them." Then he said to him, "So shall your offspring be." Abram believed the LORD, and he credited it to him as righteousness.** *Ge 15:15* **You, however, will go to your fathers in peace and be buried at a good old age.** *Ge 15:18* **On that day the LORD made a covenant with Abram and said, "To your descendants I give this land,**

Ge 17:1 When Abram was ninety-nine years old, **the LORD appeared to him and said, "I am God Almighty; walk before me and be blameless.** *Ge 17:5* **No longer will you be** called Abram ; your name will be Abraham, for I have made you a father of many nations. *Ge 17:6* **I will make you very fruitful; I will make nations of you, and kings will come from you.**

Ge 17:7 the LORD appeared to him and said, **I will establish my covenant as an everlasting covenant between me and you and your descendants after you for the generations to come, to be your God and the God of your descendants after you.** *Ge 17:8* **The whole land of Canaan, where you are now an alien, I will give as an everlasting possession to you and your descendants after you; and I will be their God." *Ge 17:9* Then God said to Abraham, "As for you, you must keep my covenant, you and your descendants after you for the generations to come. *Ge 17:10* This is my covenant with you and your descendants after you, the covenant you are to keep: Every male among you shall be circumcised. *Ge 17:11* You are to undergo circumcision, and it will be the sign of the covenant between me and you. *Ge 17:12* For the generations to come every male among you who is eight days old must be circumcised, including those born in your household or bought with money from a foreigner—those who are not your offspring. *Ge 17:13* Whether born in your household or bought with your money, they must be circumcised. My covenant in your flesh is to be an everlasting covenant. *Ge 17:14* Any uncircumcised male, who has not been circumcised in the flesh, will be cut off from his people; he has broken my covenant." *Ge 17:15* God also said to Abraham, "As for Sarai your wife,** you are no longer to call her Sarai; her name will be Sarah. *Ge 17:16* **I will bless her and will surely give you a son by her. I will bless her so that she will be the mother of nations; kings of peoples will come from her."**

Ge 18:11 **Abraham and Sarah were already old and well advanced in years, and Sarah was past the age of childbearing.**

The Birth of Isaac

Ge 21:1 **Now the LORD was gracious to Sarah as he had said, and the LORD did for Sarah what he had promised.** *Ge 21:2* **Sarah became pregnant and bore a son to Abraham in his old age, at the very time God had promised him.** *Ge 21:3* **Abraham gave the name Isaac to the son Sarah bore him.** *Ge 21:4* **When his son Isaac was eight days old, Abraham circumcised him, as God commanded him.** *Ge 21:5* **Abraham was a hundred years old when his son Isaac was born to him**. *Ge 21:6* Sarah said, "God has brought me laughter, and everyone who hears about this will laugh with me." *Ge 21:7* And she added, "Who would have said to Abraham that Sarah would nurse children? Yet I have borne him a son in his old age."

Abraham Tested

Ge 22:1 Sometime later **God tested Abraham.** He said to him, "Abraham!" "Here I am," he replied. *Ge 22:2* Then God said, "Take your son , your only son, Isaac, whom you love, and go to the region of Moriah. Sacrifice him there as a burnt offering on one of the mountains I will tell you about." *Ge 22:3* Early the next morning Abraham got up and saddled his donkey. He took with him two of his servants and his son

Isaac. When he had cut enough wood for the burnt offering, he set out for the place God had told him about. *Ge 22:4* On the third day Abraham looked up and saw the place in the distance. *Ge 22:5* He said to his servants, "Stay here with the donkey while I and the boy go over there. We will worship and then we will come back to you." *Ge 22:6* Abraham took the wood for the burnt offering and placed it on his son Isaac, and he himself carried the fire and the knife. As the two of them went on together, *Ge 22:7* Isaac spoke up and said to his father Abraham, "Father?" "Yes, my son?" Abraham replied. "The fire and wood are here," Isaac said, "but where is the lamb for the burnt offering?" *Ge 22:8* Abraham answered, "God himself will provide the lamb for the burnt offering, my son." And the two of them went on together. *Ge 22:9* When they reached the place God had told him about, Abraham built an altar there and arranged the wood on it. He bound his son Isaac and laid him on the altar, on top of the wood. *Ge 22:10* Then he reached out his hand and took the knife to slay his son. *Ge 22:11* But the angel of the LORD called out to him from heaven, "Abraham! Abraham!" "Here I am," he replied. *Ge 22:12* "Do not lay a hand on the boy," he said. "Do not do anything to him. **Now I know that you fear God**, because you have not withheld from me your son, your only son." *Ge 22:13* Abraham looked up and there in a thicket he saw a ram caught by its horns. He went over and took the ram and sacrificed it as a burnt offering instead of his son. *Ge 22:14* So Abraham called that place The LORD Will Provide. And to this day it is said, "On the mountain of the LORD it will be provided." *Ge 22:15* **The angel of the LORD called to Abraham from heaven a second time** *Ge*

²²˸¹⁶ and said, "I swear by myself, declares the LORD, that because you have done this and have not withheld your son, your only son, *Ge 22:17* I will surely bless you and make your descendants as numerous as the stars in the sky and as the sand on the seashore. Your descendants will take possession of the cities of their enemies, *Ge 22:18* and through your offspring all nations on earth will be blessed, because you have obeyed me."

Ge 26:1 Now there was a famine in the land—besides the earlier famine of Abraham's time—and Isaac went to Abimelech king of the Philistines in Gerar. *Ge 26:2* The LORD appeared to Isaac and said, "Do not go down to Egypt; live in the land where I tell you to live. *Ge 26:3* Stay in this land for a while, and I will be with you and will bless you. For to you and your descendants I will give all these lands and will confirm the oath I swore to your father Abraham. *Ge 26:4* I will make your descendants as numerous as the stars in the sky and will give them all these lands, and through your offspring all nations on earth will be blessed, *Ge 26:5* because Abraham obeyed me and kept my requirements, my commands, my decrees and my laws." *Ge 26:6* So Isaac stayed in Gerar.

Sometime later God tested St. KP Panggabean as the fourth test of his calling. The family of St. KP Panggabean was suffering the same issues as the Israel, as the prophesying at the beginning formation of the family in the wedding. There were three times when the family was facing severe famine due to economical issue at 1965-1968, 1997-2000 and year 2008-2009 in the midst of his calling (Gen.12:10; Gen.26:1; and Gen. 42-43vv). The other issue of the family is his children was hard to find their husbands and wives; even after one of his children get married, one month after the wedding, they were separated and the other son even he had their wife, he did not had the child (Gen. 11:30; Gen. 15:2; Gen.25.21; Gen.29:31) and they married in the old age (Gen.25:20). In his last days, St. KP Panggabean use his idle time to write the passage from the Bible to a book into three different languages: Batak, Indonesia and English. He never complains God for his poverty, and has no grandson. Then comes a days when he was alone, at the afternoon when dark is comes, he try to turn the street light on with a chair but unfortunately he fell down and broke his leg. Due to he was old, Theo as the firstborn daughter commands not to bring him to the hospital. She only asks mom to invite the traditional massage and ask a doctor to come to give him the medicine. The condition of St. KP Panggabean was become worse. He cries out to the Lord that he will now die and had no grandson (Gen. 15: 2). Then the third child, Ani, calls the fourth child about this for the fourth child was work in outside the Promised Land. Then the fourth child call his mom to get the father to the hospital and promise to sent the money for that. But mom refused it for in her thought the doctor will advise to surgery. Then the fourth child calls the firstborn daughter and the sixth child with the same message with the special intention: "Why do you let father cry-out in pain". In the midst of the last days of

St. KP Panggabean, there comes granddad in a dream to mom told that he wants to separate her and dad, **"naeng pasirangonhu ho dohot iananghon hi (Gen.15:15)"**. Finally due to the condition become worse, they brought St. KP Panggabean to the hospital. In the hospital there come the relatives of St. KP Panggabean both from his family line or mom's family, his teachers' colleagues, students and also the member of the church. They pray and give money. The visitor come were so continue to see and amazed the doctor, the sister and security who was St KP Panggabean exactly. And the fourth son sent the money for the initial payment and comes to visit him in the hospital for a week (Gen.48:1). The fourth son was keep dad accompanied with mom in hospital for about one week. He never went home at that time. He went directly to the hospital, and when the leave is over he went back to work from the hospital. In the hospital the doctor advise mom to take a CT scan his brain to find the cause of dad sickness. But the firstborn daughter refused it. She advises no need for her mom has told all the family about her dream. And the doctor advises as well to give additional blood to him. Then the fourth son agree to the doctor advises and went to the other hospital accompanied by the sixth child to get the blood donor bag. After **4ᵗʰ** day **the fourth son** accompanied his father at the hospital and give his father treatment, dad who was dying and lost his consciousness the day before, at **4** o'clock he woke up (Gen.49:2). This makes the doctor surprise and testifies this is because of the praying. He has treatment in the hospital about a month, and then mom decide to bring back to home and only give the medicine and invite a nurse to clean wound of flesh at his back due to too long stay in the bed. At home, in the morning before she went to the office, the third child was to wash up her father. Mom gives him food at morning, day and afternoon. And at the other occasion the seventh child who wash up her father. One day when the third child wants to clean up her father, he found that dad look emptied and quietly. She asked **did you angry and sorry that your children were not married? Dad answered no.** Then comes a day when St. KP Panggabean lying in bed, he wondered with a vision. He looked up at the surroundings of his bedroom and saw lights like the stars around his bed (Gen. 15:5). When the third child wants to wash up his body, he asks her not to hindering him from this vision in Batak language: "**Jaga jo, jaga jo**". Then her third daughter asks **why?** He said **there are lights around the bedroom.** The third daughter continued to ask **where?** Dad reply and show with his weak hand: **this around the bedroom.** The third child asks **where? There is no light here?** In other occasion when the seventh child wants to wash up him, he said the same **Jaga jo, jaga jo. Go away and do not hinder my vision. I am seeing lights around the bedroom.** When the sixth child comes to visit him and he found the same that his dad wonders with the vision. **Dad said that he saw the lights and there is a name Isaac in the vision.** They told this latter to the other childs who had not known about this repeatedly. Latter the fourth child advises that the vision is Daniel 12:3. This then carved in the dad's grave stone. **Mom also had a dream given a baby by the angel and asked her to take care the baby.** Six month after the death of dad, the sixth son Giat was married to May. Mom and the firstborn daughter asked the fourth son to pay the expenses of the wedding and Mom's golden age birthday 75 years old. The firstborn daughter was praises the fourth son for he pays the expenses and for Mom's friends praise Mom who succeed in great wedding and golden birthday party (Gen.49:8). Then two years after the death of St. KP Panggabean, mom gets her first grandson from her son at 24-12-2013, and she names him Isaac. Actually the father of May had proposed to name his grandson Joshua as descendant of Joseph. The family were rejoice and happy for the birth of Isaac. The Church members testify that Isaac looks like his granddad, and the neighbor feels that Isaac is handsome like a Western people. Isaac was the promised grandson to St. KP Panggabean, while Isaac is the promised son to Abraham. Isaac is the evidence of God's covenantal fellowship faithfulness to his chosen people. The fulfillment of God's promises in the covenant was begins in the small part of St KP Panggabean family, the weakest point. The oracle of Micah is applied in this in Mic. 5:2: "

"But you, Bethlehem Ephrathah, though you are small among the clans of Judah, out of you will come for me one who will be ruler over Israel, whose origins are from of old, from ancient times"

God credited to St. KP Panggabean as righteousness

because he believes God's covenant promises to go from his father house and found a church and receive the Promised Land without pay any money, to gain the twelve Promised Lands, and the promise of his heirs even he did not see Isaac (Gen. 15:6). The lights that St. KP Panggabean saw while his dying were his sons and daughters, his grandchildren, his descendants, the saints, the God's covenantal people includes Isaac. God said to St. KP Panggabean that he will have a promised grandson and the family would name him Isaac. Isaac was named by God through a vision for special mission to be God's servant, just like Moses, Samuel, John the Baptist, Jesus Christ, etc. The covenantal fellowship between God and St. KP Panggabean and his descendants is the same as the Abrahamic covenant. The promises that God given to St. KP Panggabean and his descendants is the same as Abrahamic covenant.

CHAPTER ELEVEN

Jacob Gets Isaac's Blessing

Ge 27:1 When Isaac was old and his eyes were so weak that he could no longer see, he called for Esau his older son and said to him, "My son." "Here I am," he answered. *Ge 27:2* Isaac said, "I am now an old man and don't know the day of my death. *Ge 27:3* Now then, get your weapons—your quiver and bow—and go out to the open country to hunt some wild game for me. *Ge 27:4* Prepare me the kind of tasty food I like and bring it to me to eat, so that I may give you my blessing before I die." *Ge 27:5* Now Rebekah was listening as Isaac spoke to his son Esau. When Esau left for the open country to hunt game and bring it back, *Ge 27:6* Rebekah said to her son Jacob, "Look, I overheard your father say to your brother Esau, *Ge 27:7* 'Bring me some game and prepare me some tasty food to eat, so that I may give you my blessing in the presence of the LORD before I die.' *Ge 27:8* Now, my son, listen carefully and do what I tell you: *Ge 27:9* Go out to the flock and bring me two choice young goats, so I can prepare some tasty food for your father, just the way he likes it. *Ge 27:10* Then take it to your father to eat, so that he may give you his blessing

before he dies." *Ge 27:11* Jacob said to Rebekah his mother, "But my brother **Esau is a hairy man**, and **I'm a man with smooth skin.** *Ge 27:12* What if my father touches me? I would appear to be tricking him and would bring down a curse on myself rather than a blessing." *Ge 27:13* His mother said to him, "My son, let the curse fall on me. Just do what I say; go and get them for me." *Ge 27:14* So he went and got them and brought them to his mother, and she prepared some tasty food, just the way his father liked it. *Ge 27:15* Then Rebekah took the best clothes of Esau her older son, which she had in the house, and put them on her younger son Jacob. *Ge 27:16* She also covered his hands and the smooth part of his neck with the goatskins. *Ge 27:17* Then she handed to her son Jacob the tasty food and the bread she had made. *Ge 27:18* He went to his father and said, "My father." "Yes, my son," he answered. "Who is it?" *Ge 27:19* Jacob said to his father, "I am Esau your firstborn. I have done as you told me. Please sit up and eat some of my game so that you may give me your blessing." *Ge 27:20* Isaac asked his son, "How did you find it so quickly, my son?" "The LORD your God gave me success," he replied. *Ge 27:21* Then Isaac said to Jacob, "Come near so I can touch you, my son, to know whether you really are my son Esau or not." *Ge 27:22* Jacob went close to his father Isaac, who touched him and said, "The voice is the voice of Jacob, but the hands are the hands of Esau." *Ge 27:23* He did not recognize him, for his hands were hairy like those of his brother Esau; so he blessed him. *Ge 27:24* "Are you really my son Esau?" he asked. "I am," he replied. *Ge 27:25* **Then he said, "My son, bring me some of your**

game to eat, so that I may give you my blessing." Jacob brought it to him and he ate; and he brought some wine and he drank. ^{Ge 27:26} Then his father Isaac said to him, "Come here, my son, and kiss me." ^{Ge 27:27} So he went to him and kissed him. When Isaac caught the smell of his clothes, he blessed him and said, "Ah, the smell of my son is like the smell of a field that the LORD has blessed. ^{Ge 27:28} May God give you of heaven's dew and of earth's richness—an abundance of grain and new wine. ^{Ge 27:29} May nations serve you and peoples bow down to you. Be lord over your brothers, and may the sons of your mother bow down to you. May those who curse you be cursed and those who bless you be blessed.

^{Ge 27:35} But he said, "Your brother came deceitfully and took your blessing." ^{Ge 27:36} Esau said, "Isn't he rightly named Jacob? He has deceived me these two times: He took my birthright, and now he's taken my blessing!" ^{Ge 27:37} Isaac answered Esau, "I have made him lord over you and have made all his relatives his servants, and I have sustained him with grain and new wine.

^{Ob 1:9} … Esau's mountains will be cut down in the slaughter. ^{Ob 1:10} Because of the violence against your brother Jacob, you will be covered with shame; you will be destroyed forever. ^{Ob 1:11} On the day you stood aloof while strangers carried off his wealth and foreigners entered his gates and cast lots for Jerusalem, you were like one of them. ^{Ob 1:12} You should not look down on your brother in the day of his misfortune, rejoice over the people of Judah in the day of their destruction, nor boast so much in the day

of their trouble. ^{Ob 1:13} You should not march through the gates of my people in the day of their disaster, nor look down on them in their calamity in the day of their disaster, nor seize their wealth in the day of their disaster.

Mal 1:2 "I have loved you," says the LORD. "But you ask, 'How have you loved us?' "Was not Esau Jacob's brother?" the LORD says. "Yet I have loved Jacob, ^{Mal 1:3} but Esau I have hated, and I have turned his mountains into a wasteland and left his inheritance to the desert jackals.

Gal 4:22 For it is written that Abraham had two sons, one by the slave woman and the other by the free woman. *Gal 4:23* His son by the slave woman was born in the ordinary way; but his son by the free woman was born as the result of a promise. *Gal 4:24* These things may be taken figuratively, for the women represent two covenants. One covenant is from Mount Sinai and bears children who are to be slaves: This is Hagar.

Ex 33:19 And the LORD said, "I will cause all my goodness to pass in front of you, and I will proclaim my name, the LORD, in your presence. I will have mercy on whom I will have mercy, and I will have compassion on whom I will have compassion. (Ro. 9:15-16). ^{Ro 9:16} It does not, therefore, depend on man's desire or effort, but on God's mercy.

Jacob Blesses His Sons

Ge 49:3 "Reuben, you are my firstborn, my might, the first sign of my strength, excelling in honor, excelling in power. *Ge 49:4* Turbulent as the waters, you will no longer excel, for you went up onto your father's bed, onto my couch and defiled it.

Ge 49:8 "Judah, your brothers will praise you; your hand will be on the neck of your enemies; your father's sons will bow down to you.

Ge 49:22 "Joseph is a fruitful vine, a fruitful vine near a spring, whose branches climb over a wall. *Ge 49:23* With bitterness archers attacked him; they shot at him with hostility. *Ge 49:24* But his bow remained steady, his strong arms stayed limber, because of the hand of the Mighty One of Jacob, because of the Shepherd, the Rock of Israel, *Ge 49:25* because of your father's God, who helps you, because of the Almighty, who blesses you with blessings of the heavens above, blessings of the deep that lies below, blessings of the breast and womb. *Ge 49:26* Your father's blessings are greater than the blessings of the ancient mountains, than the bounty of the age-old hills. Let all these rest on the head of Joseph, on the brow of the prince among his brothers.

The Death of Abraham

Ge 25:7 Altogether, **Abraham lived** a hundred and **seventy-five years**. *Ge 25:8* **Then Abraham breathed his last and died at a good old age, an old man and full of years;** and he was gathered to his people. *Ge 25:9* His sons Isaac and Ishmael buried him in the cave of Machpelah near Mamre, in the field of Ephron son of Zohar the Hittite, *Ge 25:10* the field Abraham had bought from the Hittites. There Abraham was buried with his wife Sarah. *Ge 25:11* **After Abraham's death, God blessed his son Isaac,** who then lived near Beer Lahai

Roi. *Ge 15:15* **You, however, will go to your fathers in peace and be buried at a good old age.**

One day in the morning in year 1996 when St. KP Panggabean was at home, there is a driver who drove the truck careless beside our house and hit our fence and broke. St. KP Panggabean was angry for this. The driver was a young man and raise in anger as well. He went back and asked his parents accompanied by his brother who is gangster in the traditional market and a security came home and complained at night. The firstborn daughter was met them and argue. Dad was at home as well and do not know that was because of the morning incident. For the tension of the conversation was raise, the fourth son came and try to calm down the tension. But due to the fourth son came, the brother of the driver become more angry and supposed that the man who angry with his brother is the fourth son. Two head of the neighbors came to hear the debate. And calm down the uninvited visitor that dad angry was normal because we have several times hit by the truck. Then the uninvited visitor agreed and went home. Dad stayed inside and did not know about this. But after they gone, the firstborn daughter complain to him to stay cool when talk to the stranger. The fourth son talked none. One day in the morning in 1996 there is a madman passed the street in front our house and singing and shout loudly. Dad was already woke-up and sit down in chair in front the house after take a breakfast. The madman was asking dad a cigarette. Dad replied him that he had already stopped to smoke after pension. The madman asked why? Are you stressed and mad? You want me to take you to jail? In hearing this, the fourth son who was already woke-up and sit inside the house, came out to meet them and say no to the madman, dad is not mad and no need to put him to jail. The fourth son was intended to hit the head of madman whenever he touch dad with small pottery in the terrace. But because he went out, he cancelled. After he gone, the fourth son advises dad not to talk to madman. He will think you are mad. Dad did not understand this. After we met again with the madman in front of the church, the fourth son again reminds dad that the man was madman, and do not talk with him. In our house there were always comes singer to asked money door by door. In his old age, dad cannot handle his anger especially when he heard the singer comes to our house and traditional street musical which play their instrument loudly. Sometimes dad was thrown them by stone and shout loudly to send them out. But one day when a singer with Ukulele came to sing, dad was invite to come inside using our granddad stick for the old man to support his body. And dad even was acting inviting him to fight and intend to hit the singer with the stick, while the singer want to hit dad with his Ukulele. To see this before something happened to dad, the fourth son shouted with loud voice to afraid the singer to go away and intended to go to in front our house to fight with the singer. And the singer then went away because of this voice. After his gone, the fourth son advises dad to reduce his anger and do not try to fight with young man. When the fourth son came home from his office outside the Promised Land, he always brings food to the family. And if he found that he saw is something good for dad and the family, such as t-shirt, or batik shirt, he will bought it and give to dad and the family. Dad was so happy and mom as well. Mom was also given a mixed gold and bronze by the fourth son whenever he comeback from Papua. In fact, in the past when dad was active to work, the firstborn daughter was always give money to help mother to pay bill and food. But After Heinze was born, the firstborn daughter complain and asked to reduce this because of she cannot afford it. She told that the burden is too heavy now. Therefore the fourth son agreed to help family budget. In year 2008 when Heinze grown up and his need become more intensive, she again asked to reduce it and effectively most of the source of income was handled by the fourth son with addition from the third child and the seventh child. In year 1998 mom was suffering hypothyroid cancer on her throat. Doctor said this should be taken out. Then she had a treatment in hospital for about 2 weeks in hospital. The fourth son and the fifth son were accompanied her, while the expenses were paid by the firstborn daughter and her husband Wang. Since year 2000 after dad pension his healthy was become worse. He suffered heart attack and artery plugged. He was fall down when the heart attacked. Then he had several treatments at the hospital. The fourth son advises that all children should contribute to dad budget for treatment and medicine, even he or she only can give small amount. This is about 1 million rupiahs per month. But because we are only low staff, we cannot afford. The second son can only able to give a small amount for several months only, and also the fifth son who are not work. Therefore the fourth son gave more than the others with addition from the third child and the sixth son and the seventh child. Mom was happy that the children collect money for dad. This appreciation was even testifies at church or family gathering. Even when the fourth son is not work for his contract was end, when dad was asking money for collection in Church, He gives dad money. The fourth son is not only gave his money to take care dad. When the heart attack came, the fourth son was quickly wake and heard the situation and give dad medicine to cure. One day his finger bitten by dad when he attempt to put medicine in dad mouth. He is the first one to hear when he was at home for he was sleep earlier than the other because he was like watching soccer that lives on TV at the early morning. Heart attack was usually comes in the early morning, but sometime at middle of the night. At his idle time, when he was no contract of work, the fourth son was accompanied dad come and back to the church by walk. When he was able to buy the motorcycle, he accompanied dad to go and back from the church by motorcycle. The second child was argued that he was busy with trumpet in the church, therefore that he was usually handle this asked the fourth son to take care dad. The fifth son who cannot afford to buy the motorcycle, he always asks the fourth son to borrow the motorcycle. There comes a Sunday when the fifth son asks to borrow the motorcycle. He promised to take dad go and back the church, while the fourth son by walk. At the first time he meet with his promised, but at the other occasion he was busy with his business and forgot to take dad back from the church. The fourth son was so hardly take care dad went back home from the church by walk because dad was so old and cannot walk too far, even 100meter. He will lose control of his body and fell down if too far walk. This was not despised by the fifth son. When he came after he finished his business, the fourth son complained and angry with him for several times. Dad was 70 years old at that time. He cannot walk far. But the firstborn daughter advises that this is because dad was too lazy to sit at home therefore gradually become weak fast. Therefore she and aunt advises dad to practice walk each day. One day dad tried to practice this. But unfortunately, beside our house he cannot able to stabilize her body and fall down. He hurt at hands and legs. And the neighbor was found him down and scream. Therefore we go take dad and bring back home. The fourth son takes care and treat dad, buy the medicine and give dad treatment. But because the hurts was not cured, the fourth son bring him to a small clinic near house by becak, traditional bicycle. Then mom called the firstborn daughter about this. The fourth son was angry and blamed the firstborn daughter for this. In the other occasion, dad plans to check his health in a lab near houses or at the hospital to consult the heart specialist doctor. The fourth son was accompanied him to check his health to a small clinic or hospital by becak or by taxi when the fourth son can afford the payment. But when the fourth son is unable to pay taxi or becak, he will ask public transportation that was on the street near the house. These were happened for several times. The fourth son sometimes cries in his deepest heart pray to God for this heavy burden to take care dad in his old time and in his Poor. Even the fourth son in his poor must taken cared dad. He eventually compared to the other member of the church whose God gave them blessing more than God given to dad and his family. But the fourth son is not complained to the others to handle the duty to take care dad. Those historical events were not realized by the fourth son, the firstborn daughter, the first son who is the second child and the other sons and daughters. **The more they pay time and money to give to dad and the family, the more the possibility to get blesses of the firstborn son. The more they involve to protect and to secure dad and the family, the more the possibility to get blesses of the firstborn son (Gen. 34: 30 and 35:3-5 compare to Gen. 37: 26 and Gen. 44: 18). The more they obey the Commandment and the Law of God, The more the possibility to get the firstborn son's blessings (Gen. 39: 8-10 compare to Gen. 49:4-5). For God had blessed St. KP Panggabean (Gen. 12: 1-2) and God bless his wife and his descendants (Gen. 17:16; 25:11) and St. KP Panggabean then would give the firstborn son's blessing to those who give him and his family food and protection (Gen. 27:4) and that blessing**

will down through his generation (Gen. 17: 16; 27:27-29 and Gen. 49:9-12; 22-26ff). But in fact it is only by God's grace and election and Predestined, nothing else. Actually this is automatically the duty of the firstborn daughter to give dad and whole family food and protect them so they would prosper, safe, and secure. The firstborn daughter should be automatically to be the instrument of God's blessing to the Family of Israel. Because she has beauty, smart, wise and excellent in speak, think and acting. But she despised all of this and let the fourth son to take over her duties. In fact, all of the family of Israel should keep the covenant law, the Torah, that none of them to inter marry with pagan and commit adultery. These were despised again by the firstborn daughter.

The fifth son is some kind like Joseph, the firstborn son of Rachel. He might be not feed the family of St. KP Panggabean but he involve in protect them. He had challenge Tolut to fight when Tolut angry to him for he return back money from the diakonia when dad was treated in hospital. He also threat Rev Roma not to make riot in his father church. One day he hit a son of an elder who was friend of Tolut, for he had play card in his father church. When Mom was in hospital in year 1998 and year 2001 he accompanied mom. When the fourth son was sick as well he accompanied. And also when the third child was in hospital, he accompanied her. Even when Aunt Ready was in hospital, he has accompanied her in three times in different occasions. One day when He and Aunt Ready went to Pansurnapitu to see granddad and grandma, the fifth son protect aunt Ready from attacking bee who suspected sent from someone to attack Aunt Ready. The fifth son suffers in sickness for about three days for this. When they went back home, Aunt Ready told this to dad and say thank. Aunt Ready was alone, her husband now is dead and she had no child of her own. Therefore according to Batak social-cultural law, she had to get back to the family. She is now under our father responsibility. Therefore the fifth son got also the blessing of the firstborn son that had been divided into the fourth son of Leah (Judah) and the son of Rachel: Joseph. Therefore Jacob blessed his son Ephraim and his descendant: Joshua son of Nun.

St. KP Panggabean was fall down from the chair when he tried to light up the street lamp. His serious illness became worse. Then the fourth son called his mom, the firstborn daughter and the sixth son to bring him to the hospital and sent money for the first payment. One week in the hospital, the firstborn daughter call the fourth son about the sickness of dad that become worse, even dying and lost of his consciousness and that mom had a dream met with our grand dad that bring the message want to separate her with his son. The firstborn daughter was told this to the fourth son. Then the fourth son asks his boss to get on leave for a week to see his dad (Gen.48:1). The fourth son was keep dad accompanied with mom in hospital for about one week. He never went home at that time. He went directly to the hospital, and when the leave is over he went back to work from the hospital. The fifth son and his friend May accompanied as well in hospital about one night. At hospital when St. KP Panggabean was lost his consciousness, the fourth son read him a Psalm passage 23-25vv and Rom. 1-3vv and Eph.1-3vv. The doctor was advises to the fourth son to buy some additional medicines, to take brain scan and get transfusion blood. The fourth son agreed with the doctor. But in the afternoon the firstborn daughter was told that it is no need to brain scan and blood transfusion. The firstborn daughter was told this for mom told that she had met with grandpa in a dream that he want to separate dad and mom. But these are already prepared by the fourth son. The firstborn daughter was also rejected to wash up and clean dad. This was told by the third child. The third child wonder why she reject it, cause he was his daddy not someone else. But later the firstborn daughter accompanied with the fourth son and the second son were clean up and wash the feces of dad. The miracle was happened. After blood transfusion and additional mixed medicine, Dad which before the fourth son came was dying and lost his consciousness, back to his healthy and woke up in the morning at 4 o'clock, at day 4th **the fourth son** accompanied him (Gen. 48:2). He can hear the voice of window sheet that opened by the fourth son and even ask: "Do this **Judah Ministry** Hospital (means: the service or dedication of Judah—the fourth son of Jacob/Israel)? And ask do this restroom?" At the day fifth of accompanied by the fourth son, St. KP Panggabean was become better than yesterday. He also woke up at 4 o'clock. The fourth son wonder with dad dress prepared in his treatment room. The firstborn daughter perhaps had a math logic. She had prepared dad dress for him in the case he breaths his last at hospital. They planned that after he breaths his last, soon mom will asks doctor to wash the body perfumed and inject formaline and to use his good dress before the body become stiffness. But the fourth son has a faith logic. He would do anything that he could do to serve his dad as long as he lives. And miracles happened. When the firstborn asks the fourth son how about the condition of dad now, she wonders that dad get well back after lost his consciousness. One day the firstborn daughter was praises the fourth son who take good care dad in the hospital, and God gives dad recover his health (Gen.49:8). And sister at the hospital told the recover health of St. KP Panggabean to the doctor and doctor testifying this is because of the prayer of visitors to the fourth son. At the end of the week the second son asks the fourth son to **help the father eat and drink milk, and medicine (Gen.27:25).** Before the fourth son went back to his work, he was intended to hold and kiss his dad, but he was doubt. But suddenly the second son asked the fourth son **to hold dad and kiss him (Gen 27:27).** This event was not realized by the fourth son. But after event by event and mom keep prophesying that our suffering is some kind like Israel, the fourth son come to understanding this historical event has the same with the Bible story with variation and in a very tiny scale.

In his diaspora, the fourth son was always praying at the morning for our dad health, and if God's will is to take him, please forgive his iniquity and sent his spirit to God. He also calls mom regularly to ask about dad condition and advise mom stay faithfully to accompanied dad in his last days and lead him in pray. Our relative and the member of the church came to visit him, pray and also give money. His students which had been taught 25 years ago come as well to pray and give money to him. Therefore for 1 month in hospital and 5 months treatment at home, most of the payment for his illness is paid from our relatives, his students and the church. In the future, the fourth son has been calculated it the total money given when his father was sick is about 100 million rupiah about US $10,000. He has been brought to the hospital with four doctor take care him for about 1 month. After this mom decide to bring back to home to take care by herself and invite one sister near our home to clean up his wound due to too long stay at bed. When he celebrated his birthday 76 years of age, he celebrated it at his bedroom. He had been in bed for about six months. Then comes a day when one of head of the family a member of our church proposed that when one of pioneer of the church is suffering hard sickness, the whole church should be give him the money offering as thanks giving. The head of the church Rev Simson ask mom about this and she said I need to ask her children. Then she asked all the children especially the firstborn daughter who is in her sight is the head of the children and had been give her money and attention to the whole family. But she can't find the right answer from them, include from the firstborn daughter. The firstborn girl was unable to decide it. Finally mom called the fourth son who worked outside the Promised Land about this. The fourth son insist agree with the proposed and ask his mom to receive it. After six month treatment then comes a day at November 2011 when money that kept by mom was indicated empty and cannot able to buy medicine for further treatment. Then she asks the firstborn daughter about this. Again, the firstborn daughter give it up cannot handle this. Then mom decided to asks to the fourth son who worked outside the Promised Land. And the fourth son replied yes I am able to continue to give money for dad treatment. A couple days later, about the end of November 2011, St. KP Panggabean asks the third child who always accompanied him in her idle time to call the fourth son who worked outside the Promised Land. Next two days he asked the third child as well to call the fourth son again. After calling the fourth son asked the third child what was the conversation? He asked this because dad speaks become so weak and cannot understand what he said. In the future when mom again prophesying our family suffering like Israel to commemorate his dead, then he concluded that **the two calls was blessing for the firstborn son**. It is indicated with the birth of the fourth son which is 1st -12, that symbolically elected to be the firstborn of the twelve tribes of Israel (Gen.27:29, 37; 49:8). While the firstborn daughter who despised his birthright become the last of the twelve (12th -12 compare to Gen. 27:40; 49:3-4), for she is the firstborn daughter had failed to feed and kept the father and all the family; and beside she was married to pagan. When December 1, the day of the birthday of the fourth son, the family celebrate it with buy food. Then St. KP Panggabean eat the food helped by his sixth son's wife July and ask her why he eat the special food? The wife of the sixth son replied for the birthday of your favorite son, the fourth son. So as Isaac bless Jacob not Esau, and as Jacob bless Judah for he had bravely protect the all family (Gen.44:18-34) and Jacob bless Joseph for he had feed his father and all of family of Israel (Gen.50:20-21). The duty of the firstborn son to feed the father and all the family that should be upon Esau and Reuben had been despised and replaced by the younger Jacob and Judah and Joseph. The covenant law that given by the Almighty God (El-Shaddai) had been despised by Esau who married to pagan (Gen. 26:34) and Reuben who commit adultery (Gen.35:22). Therefore the bless right as the firstborn son came to Jacob the younger, Judah the fourth son who protect his brothers (Gen. 37:26-27; Gen. 43:8-9; Gen. 44:32-34) and advised his brother not to kill Joseph but save him with sold him to the pagan to be a slave, thus work outside the Promised Land (Gen. 39:1-23 and 45:5-7 and 50:20) that he could give food to his father and all the family of Israel (Gen.50:20-21). Judah also protects Benjamin (Gen. 43: 8-9; Gen. 44:32-34). Judah and Joseph is the instrument of God to bring his promise fulfilled for the family of Israel by kept them secure, safe and enough food. The firstborn child is no longer the first one for he is despised his duties (Gen. 49:3-4). Thus all of Bible story was fulfilled in the family of St.

KP Panggabean, but in variation and in a very tiny scale. It is like a puzzle. One by one of the picture is reconstructed by the author from the Church history book written by St KP Panggabean and the story of the family told by mom until it find the complete picture of the family story. And the whole family were also contribute in reconstruction the historical events. When they were gathering after dad funeral, they memorizing the last days of their father.

St. KP Panggabean has been in bed about six months after fall in. In the suffering he asks God: **"Di dia Ho Debata? Where are you God?"** In 5th December 2011 at the morning as usually the third child was washing up him. After that she went to her office. About 10.00 in the morning mom gave him food. Before eat, she leaded the prayer and dad repeated her prayer. The fourth son had told mom to accompanied him and lead the prayer in his last days. After prayer dad eat. When finish to eat, **he give thanks to mom.** And mom gives him the water. But **Dad was took his last breath and death and suddenly the angel closes his eyes and mouth.** They do not need to closes his eyes and his mouth for it already closed. Mom cries a loud and bitterly and asked the neighbor to call all children about this and also our close relatives. Mom said to the neighbors that dad does need not to wash his body for it already washed by the third child. But Mom with the neighbors changes his shirt with good dress and with his Church leader elder's shirt (Guru Huria shirt). Traditional Batak ceremony of mourning and church Funeral have been discussed that will be used the church.

The firstborn daughter was asked the fourth son to lend money for this and transfer it, before he went to church, for funeral expenses. The fourth son was asked his boss to have a mourning and funeral about a month (Gen. 50:3-7). And they await for the fourth son come from his office outside The Promised Land before the funeral. When the fourth son come to church to see his dad for the last time, all the brothers and sisters come to the door to meet the fourth son and to hold him include Heinze (Gen. 37:7,9; 42:6; 43:26,28) and after that he come to death body of St. KP Panggabean and cry with aloud voice. But Aunt Ready was asked him to shake hand, and Sudung cry with aloud voice in aunt's shoulder and then came to mother and his lamented loudly and bitterly (10v). The fourth son was asked by the firstborn daughter to lead to bring the box of St. KP Panggabean to Church elders with the picture of dad in his hands. The fourth son actually asked Heinze to accompany him to bring the cross of his granddad name but he refused it. And He also asked by the firstborn daughter to pay all of the funeral expenses (Gen. 50:1-14). Mom testifies in the funeral that in his last days, dad gain the fruits of his good works in ministering, preaching, advising and caring the people, the Church member, relatives, neighbors, friends and his students. They feel bless and thanks to his ministering and teaching (Gen. 12:2). It was good lesson learning for all the audiences she continues. Ingkon jolo dirasahon pamanganna sude angka ulaonna na denggani dungi laho ma Ibana. Before he died, he must taste his fruits of his good works. They were gathered in his treatment at hospital and at houses and at his funeral at Church and give him money for his treatment and funeral expenses. When he was a teacher, St KP Panggabean said to the fourth son that he was succeed to lead his students passed with minimum graded, while the other teachers failed. July also testified that her relatives, one of his colleagues teacher said that his attitude is good and don't want gather with other teachers to talk about issues and gossips. The fourth son also testified that dad was unique than the other teachers for he likes gathering with his students and talks kidding. His relatives also thanks to him for he had ministering and help them to be a good Christian. Then Rev Simson blesses St. KP Panggabean in the Church before buried. Rev Simson preaches at the pulpit to the audiences, his relatives and Church member, that the Church is St KP Panggabean's great work. He was the founder of the Church. St. KP Panggabean then was buried on his family burial site. He was buried above his father bone (Gen.15:15 ; 35:29 and 49:29).

In the New Year's eve commemoration after the death of St. KP Panggabean, the fourth son still commit to protect mom and feed mom and give his money to others and to pay their need for married (Gen. 50:20-21). A year after this when mom was home alone, a son of the second son's closest friend was deceived him to steal his keyboard electronic organ. We come to his home to ask to return the keyboard. He denies he stole the keyboard. But because we do not have other witness, we cannot able to put him to jail. Then the fourth son arranges to install CCTV to protect mom whenever she was home alone. The thief even tried to deceive the second son for the second time. He tries to steal home for second time, but failed or might be postponed for there is CCTV installed. Mom was old now, she was 77 years old now. She suffer her knees was hurt when she wants to bend. She then told this to her children. The firstborn daughter asked to check to the doctor. She went to the doctor accompanied by the third child. The doctor advised to inject the liquid five times. Mom was worried about the expenses. The fourth son advises and give her opinion to follow the doctor advises. Now mom would bend without hurt, walk like a young woman even in his oldiest.

CHAPTER TWELVE

Jacob Flees To Laban

Ge 27:41 **Esau held a grudge against Jacob because of the blessing his father had given him.** He said to himself, "The days of mourning for my father are near; **then I will kill my brother Jacob.**" *Ge 27:42* When **Rebekah was told what her older son Esau had said, she sent for her younger son Jacob and said to him, "Your brother Esau is consoling himself with the thought of killing you.** Ge 27:43 **Now then, my son, do what I say: Flee at once to my brother Laban in Haran.** Ge 27:44 **Stay with him for a while until your brother's fury subsides.** Ge 27:45 **When your brother is no longer angry with you and forgets what you did to him, I'll send word for you to come back from there.** Why should I lose both of you in one day?" *Ge 27:46* Then Rebekah said to Isaac, "I'm disgusted with living because of these Hittite women. If Jacob takes a wife from among the women of this land, from Hittite women like these, my life will not be worth living." *Ge 28:1* **So Isaac called for Jacob and blessed him and commanded him: "Do not marry a Canaanite woman.** Ge 28:2 **Go at once to Paddan Aram, to the house of your mother's father Bethuel. Take a wife** for yourself there, from among the daughters of Laban, your mother's brother. ^{Ge 28:3} May God Almighty bless you and make you fruitful and increase your numbers until you become a community of peoples. ^{Ge 28:4} May he give you and your descendants the blessing given to Abraham, so that you may take possession of the land where you now live as an alien, the land God gave to Abraham." ^{Ge 28:5} Then Isaac sent Jacob on his way, and he went to Paddan Aram, to Laban son of Bethuel the Aramean, the brother of Rebekah, who was the mother of Jacob and Esau.

^{Ge 28:20} Then Jacob made a vow, saying, "If God will be with me and will watch over me on this journey I am taking and will give me food to eat and clothes to wear ^{Ge 28:21} so that I return safely to my father's house, then the LORD will be my God ^{Ge 28:22} and this stone that I have set up as a pillar will be God's house, and of all that you give me I will give you a tenth."

Exodus: conquering of the Promised Land begin

^{Nu 13:3} So at the LORD'S command Moses sent them out from the Desert of Paran. All of them were leaders of the Israelites. from the tribe of **Judah**, Caleb son of Jephunneh. from the tribe of Ephraim, (a tribe of **Joseph**), Hoshea son of Nun. ^{Nu 13:16} These are the names of the men Moses sent to explore the land. (Moses gave Hoshea son of Nun the name **Joshua**.) When Moses sent them to explore Canaan, he said, "Go up through the Negev and on into the hill country. See what the land is like and **whether the people who live there are strong or weak, few or many.** What

kind of land do they live in? Is it good or bad? What kind of towns do they live in? Are they unwalled or fortified? How is the soil? Is it fertile or poor? Are there trees on it or not? Do your best to bring back some of the fruit of the land." (It was the season for the first ripe grapes.) So they went up and explored the land from the Desert of Zin as far as Rehob, toward Lebo Hamath.

They came back to Moses and Aaron and the whole Israelite community at Kadesh in the Desert of Paran. There they reported to them and to the whole assembly and showed them the fruit of the land. *Nu 13:27* They gave Moses this account: "We went into the land to which you sent us, and it does flow with milk and honey! Here is its fruit. *Nu 13:28* But the people who live there are powerful, and the cities are fortified and very large. We even saw descendants of Anak there. *Nu 13:29* The Amalekites live in the Negev; the Hittites, Jebusites and Amorites live in the hill country; and the Canaanites live near the sea and along the Jordan." *Nu 13:30* Then Caleb silenced the people before Moses and said, "We should go up and take possession of the land, for we can certainly do it." *Nu 13:31* But the men who had gone up with him said, "We can't attack those people; they are stronger than we are." *Nu 13:32* And they spread among the Israelites a bad report about the land they had explored. They said, "The land we explored devours those living in it. All the people we saw there are of great size. *Nu 13:33* We saw the Nephilim there (the descendants of Anak come from the Nephilim). We seemed like grasshoppers in our own eyes, and we looked the same to them." *Nu 14:6* **Joshua** son of Nun

and Caleb son of Jephunneh, who were among those who had explored the land, tore their clothes *Nu 14:7* and said to the entire Israelite assembly, "The land we passed through and explored is exceedingly good. *Nu 14:8* If the LORD is pleased with us, he will lead us into that land, a land flowing with milk and honey, and will give it to us. *Nu 14:9* Only do not rebel against the LORD. And do not be afraid of the people of the land, because we will swallow them up. Their protection is gone, but the LORD is with us. Do not be afraid of them." *Nu 14:10* But the whole assembly talked about stoning them. Then the glory of the LORD appeared at the Tent of Meeting to all the Israelites.

Now St. KP Panggabean was rest in his family burial site in his good old age (Gen.15:15). Six month after the death of dad, the mother of May, wife of the fifth son, was dead. The fourth son was on leave at that time so that he could come to visit the family in mourning. The Aunt Ready accompanied by all family came to the family mourning. But she was weak because of she was suffering serious illness heart cancer above stadium. Therefore the fourth son and the seventh child Anna hold her to go to family mourning. To see the situation, the firstborn daughter decides that all family in their turn to accompanied aunt in her last days. She lives alone in his last days. We have promised dad before he died to kept mom, and aunt in their spare lives. Aunt Ready was live alone. She had no husband anymore who had passed away and she had no child as well. According to the Batak social-cultural law, she had to went back to her family. She must be under our dad family protection. Therefore all family members include mom, wife of fifth son and wife of sixth son accompany her. But the fourth son unable to accompany her in her last days due to he must work in diaspora, outside the Promised Land. In fact, he had accompany her before when aunt was suffer soft heart attack and fall down and hurt and blood clogging. Aunt had been treatment in hospital about a week. At that time the fourth son are in his spare time. In the other occasion aunt had been treatment in hospital about three times. And the fifth son was accompanied her in the hospital when he was single. In her last days aunt was always ask the third child to call the fourth son because she was missed him. When aunt was active in work, dad always ask someone of his children to accompany her, include the second son, the fourth son, the fifth son, the sixth son and the daughter, the seventh child. But mom wondered to aunt why no one meet with her love as a step mother to them? When the second son got work and got his first salary, Aunt Ready was wonder how the second son could not buy her a kilogram of mangoes. When the fourth son went back from his diaspora, working outside the Promised Land, he brings aunt and dad and mom gifts of food from his diaspora. Aunt Ready was happy and likes the gifts. After dad was serious illness and had an accident, Aunt Ready was seem like to hide from us and tried to make her own way to separate from us. This was makes the firstborn daughter angry and influenced her brother and sister to dislike Aunt Ready. At the wedding of Giat and May, the family was prepared the family choir to be presented at the wedding at the church. They asked our dad family from Jambi to join the choir. But Aunt Ready was not involved. The firstborn daughter was argued that Aunt Ready might be rejected to join it. After the wedding, Aunt Ready was angry with us and said: marendei hamu, ndang dohot ahu, means: you are all singing in Family choir but you are not asked me to join in.

They were accompanied aunt for about 2 weeks after they saw aunt was so week. Then they felt they cannot handle this for a long time. Therefore the firstborn daughter decides to ask aunt to move to Depok, buy a second house near our home so that we can accompany her. I don't know exactly about aunt feeling. But she said agree with one condition she asked to await the fourth son to back from his diaspora before she sells the house. The firstborn daughter asks the fourth son when you coming back? The fourth son was not sure about this and therefore the firstborn daughter decide to start announce the house to sell. The fourth had suggested the minimum price that he thought proper.

Then comes a man named Ebed Torah (means servant of the Scripture) who is comes from a tribe near our country from Mt. Penabung. His tribe was relative of our tribes. He was looks good, handsome and rich. The impression was so attracting. He wants to buy the house. The transaction was with aunt and accompanied with the firstborn daughter. They agree with the price Rp 800 million rupiahs amount US$ 80,000. He lives around the house but he wants another house for parking his car. He gives aunt down payment Rp 60 million amount US$6,000. The transaction was internal without outside witnesses. Ebed was asking the firstborn daughter as the family to provide the letters such evidence from the court that our family was has the rights as her inheritance. The firstborn daughter was agreed. Then the firstborn daughter assigned a lawyer to set the letter inheritance from the court. She said that she cannot have enough time to set the letter and also the others. Ebed was asked also that we must involve the second husband family of aunt in this business transaction. Aunt was so become weak and decreasing her health day after day. She was conductor of Women Choir and Widow Choir "Naomi" in a big Church. One night before she breaths her last, she heard visitors knocking the doors and asked the seventh child to see and asks them to come in. She said bereng jo diluar ro tamu, buka jo pintu. But the seventh child was didn't find anyone else outside home. In the future the seventh child told this to the others and all agree that was the angel comes to pick up her. This means that aunt was ready to pick up by the angel. At the last day mom and the second son were in turn to accompany aunt. Then she breaths hardly and smoothly and finally she breath her last. Mom, the firstborn daughter and the second son accompany her husband family to bring her body to the family burial site at her husband's country. Mom was asked by her second husband family to give her last traditional sheet cover in the box, ulos, and testifying she must be death in her suffering home where she sent away by her husband and the place where she lost her only son. And mom continue testify that she was death in her hands, and clean her and use her best dress for burial.

About the selling of the house, Ebed was in fact had been contact and persuade the local government around aunt house from the lowest to the highest so that we are unable to get the letter of inheritance. Ebed was also blow the issue to the neighbors, the false witness and the local government, that due to we are not our aunt sons and daughters, therefore we are not have right to own aunt's house and they have the opportunity to occupy it. In facing this fact, the fourth son was angry with the firstborn daughter. He also ask why you agree with low price? The firstborn daughter argued that the house is not having certificate and besides aunt had agreed. They begin in high tension and loose in relation. In the family discussion, the firstborn daughter asked who will lead to continue the transaction. The third child supports the firstborn daughter for she admires her. The sixth son also said he prefer to lead by the firstborn daughter, for he had no time to take care this issue. She said give-up with the situation. In the midst of this situation, Ebed was tricky and persuade the firstborn daughter to give him the key of the house for he had to park his car and the brother of him wants to celebrate his married. The firstborn daughter was not suspicious and asked the fifth son to give him the key. To know this the fourth son asks the fifth son: why you give the key to him? And why you obey your sister command without thinking the consequences? The firstborn daughter might be inspired by her husband family philosophy that the buyer is the King, therefore the seller must serve the buyer all things that the king asks. With this, the Ebed occupy the Land and the House. He then assigned his driver to live in aunt home. He said to the firstborn daughter the driver was his brother. Ebed advises to involve the second husband family of aunt is his tricky as well in order that we fight with them, he inspired by the Netherland Company strategy when occupy Indonesia: devide et impera, divided the enemy with initiated internal fight among them that weakened them then occupied, and in the first they come nicely acting like to trade with Indonesia but finally conquered the land and the house was occupied by him. He also asks his servants and the labor and freeman around the house to set his equipment such as kitchen appliances and tools, knife, spoon, fork, etc and bed. He set them to illustrate that he was using the house. He also hang un-used shirt in the back of the house to dry in say that a man was lives in the house. He also proclaims to the neighbor and his relatives that he was the owner of the house for he had bought it. Even his mom was plant many kinds of plantation in front of the house. Ebed perhaps thought we are not aunt inheritance for we are not her children. He even believes that he has the right to own the house for he had gave the first payment. So he thought by the death of Aunt Ready, he felt bless to get the big house in Jakarta with only US $6,000.

Then comes a day when the fifth son came to visit

his father in law, the father of May. He passing the house and found a shop in the house and take a photo. Then he called the fourth son who had been come from the diaspora. The fourth son had a dream before he came back from Diaspora met with his father. Right after he come to house in Depok, the fourth son asked the fifth son the description of Ebed and the driver look like. The fifth son replied they were not so frightening (Nu. 14:9). We could fight with them. The fourth son convinces this was a small believe enough for the battle. When the fourth son asked mom and the second son about the house problem, mom and the second son said that Ebed was threat that he will call the police if we protest it and even take to the court and taken us to jail (Gen. 39:20). The firstborn daughter even describes that Ebed was a lawyer, his education was master in law, and rich, so you cannot able to fight him (compare this description with Nu.13:27-28 and 31-33). Then we come to the house at the next day to spy (note: this event look like the same event when Moses assigned two spies, Joshua, Hoshea son of Nun, descendant of Joseph and Ephraim; and Caleb, the descendant of Judah Nu. 13:3-30) and take photo in the morning and discuss with the uncle in law, the father of May. We decide to come to the lowest government to ask the condition. The local government invites Ebed to explain the situation. Ebed explains that the shop was his relatives. He said further that he had business transaction with aunt and asked the firstborn daughter to provide the letter of inheritance from the court. He argues that he needed the letter for he is confused to whom he must pay the rest of the money: to the first family of aunt or to the second or to ours. The fourth son understands that this means that he doesn't accept that we are the inheritance of aunt house. The fourth son and the fifth son angry and push him to give back the key of the house and the shop should be closed. Ebed don't want to give back the key. And he feels under pressure. And he asked his wife to the police. But police said they can't do it. But if we want to go to the police office to mediate, they will. The fourth son was prophesying to Ebed that he cannot be won in this battle for we are son of St KP Panggabean, a servant of God. Then we go there and we make an agreement that the house to be emptied and the key given to the local government as Ebed side. And we have to provide the letter that asked by Ebed. Then we go home. The next day he calls the firstborn daughter who is the man using white shirt (the fourth son was using it when met him). And he said that he wants to cancel the transaction. He made conversation with the fifth son as well by sms and asks his down payment back. The next two days, when we saw that the house is empty, we decide to enter the house, the fourth son and the fifth son. We have been prepared the tools, the equipment for conquering the Land and war. We also buy chains to bind the steel fence and locked. We clean and repair the house for it has been not use for more than one year. The house condition was something like an old-haunted house on the mysterious movies. It is very frightening. However, the first ex-husband of aunt has his family name same with the family name of grandma of mom. So we could call him as Tulang rorobot, uncle of mom. But they had separated way. This event some kind like the story Jacob rescue to his uncle house Laban. In fact, Silaban is the son of Sihombing in Batak tribes forefather genealogies, the uncle of mom. We then reject all the negotiation with Ebed. The equipment and the tools that was inside the house, we collect them and put outside the house. Now Ebed assigned Candu to negotiate with us. Candu said was the same with Ebed did. Candu said boasa hita halak Batak marbadai? Why we people of Batak fight? (means: why we are brother fighting? Compare: Gen.13:8). Ebed acts like Lot who wants to coup Abraham, to occupy the Promised Land. He don't bother that the Land was already given to Abraham and his descendants. He doesn't fear God anymore who is the owner of the Land who given to Abraham for his properties. He sent his herdsmen to fight. When they realize that their equipment was taken out from the house, they came and take photo. Thus the fourth son called the fifth son to be ready. The fifth son came to meet them and shout. The fourth son was screaming and cursing Candu with a wooden stick act like David to Goliath as the Spirit whispered him. The false witness that picked up from the neighbors led by the wife of lowest government was laughs. Thus Candu calls police and asks us to arrest and sent out us from the house. They thought they were transaction with aunt and now aunt dead and we are not her Inheritance. Therefore Ebed has the rights of the house and they had put their used equipment and tools inside the house. But police refuse their arguments and said that the equipment should take out from the house and let us live in the house.

Ebed then call the firstborn daughter and He wants the firstborn to lead back the transaction and argue she was in the first transaction. The fourth son did not agree for Ebed was tricky and he feels the firstborn was so weak in faith. The fourth son also had information from the neighbor that the price was too cheap, according to them, 100m^2 worth 500 million rupiahs, amount US$ 50,000; while the house has 300m^2. This was raising the firstborn daughter angry. She still feels not guilty that the problem comes due to her openness and weakness in allowing Ebed to control the negotiation. The firstborn said now we are separated and the fourth son said to her in anger you are as the head of family should protect us not destroying our family. This was makes the fourth son amazed why she weak and easy under oppressed the Stranger. Before the fourth son was suspected Ebed was using paranormal to make the firstborn daughter under control him. But latter the fourth son went back to the event when the firstborn daughter got married with pagan. She was like rebellious Esau and commit adultery and inter marry with pagan. Esau descendant, Herod, was cooperate and assigned by the oppressor Roman Emperor to occupy the Promised Land of Israel. After this the fourth son comes to the final understanding about what happen to the family of St. KP Panggabean. As to the formation of the family, the family of St. KP Panggabean was some kind like Israel in the Bible who was suffering famine, struggle in having their spouse, struggle in bearing a child, oppressed by the pagan, conquering the land, struggle in heirs, rebellious and disobedience the covenant law of God. Even though dad is not a big man, a well known leader or pastor or evangelist or arch bishop of a big church or political leader, But God had promise in the Bible that He was faithful to his people, the descendants of St. KP Panggabean, for he has faithful and obey God as his servant. Now the land was under the authority of the Fourth son. Ebed cannot find way to occupy back the land. The local government and the neighbors, the false witnesses, cannot help him and also the court and the police. Even in December 5th, 2014 he sent gangster consists of 50 people assigned by Ebed to kill the fourth son and occupy the land but he found undone on his mission (Gen. 27:29; 49:8-10, 23-24). The sixth son and his wife, July, called the police to arrest them. At the New Year celebration January 2nd, 2015, Mom insists that the fourth son and the firstborn daughter get back in good relationship, otherwise she would back to our forefather house, Pansurnapitu. The first born daughter argues and cries for the fourth son had hurt her and said that she was not received the firstborn blessing (Gen, 27:38). May with Isaac comes and hold the firstborn daughter for she had cried loudly. The third child also wept and the fifth son comes to close also and wept with his sister, they were wept together and then the fourth son came threw his arm and embraced the firstborn daughter's neck (Gen. 33:4). The fourth son insists also that he don't want leaded again by the firstborn daughter in the other occasion. The third child remains cannot receive the fourth son to lead her and the whole family. She prefers support the firstborn daughter and stay faithfully under her subordinate. She despises the fourth son ability to lead the whole family, even she despises and hates all her brothers and sometime she argue with her brothers for a small issues and fight and cries. The third child was act like the firstborn daughter and intended to reign over her brothers and rule them (Gen. 37:8,10). For this treatment, the fourth son hate her all the more and could not speak a kind word to her, even he speaks sarcastic words (Gen. 37:4).

CHAPTER THIRTEEN

Jacob Blesses His Sons

^{Ge 49:1} **Then Jacob called for his sons and said: "Gather around** so I can tell you what will happen to you in days to come. ^{Ge 49:2} **"Assemble and listen, sons of Jacob; listen to your father Israel.** ^{Ge 49:3} **"Reuben, you are my firstborn**, my might, the first sign of my strength, excelling in honor, excelling in power. ^{Ge 49:4} Turbulent as the waters, **you will no longer excel, for you went up onto your father's bed, onto my couch and defiled it.** ^{Ge 49:5} **"Simeon and Levi are brothers—their swords are weapons of violence.** ⋯ for they have …anger, so fierce, and their fury, so cruel! … ^{Ge 49:8} **"Judah, your brothers will praise you; your hand will be on the neck of your enemies; your father's sons will bow down to you**. ⋯ "Zebulun will live by the seashore and become a haven for ships; his border will extend toward Sidon. "Issachar is a rawboned donkey lying down between two saddlebags. When he sees how good is his resting place and how pleasant is his land, he will bend his shoulder to the burden and submit to forced labor

Joseph is a fruitful vine, a fruitful vine near a spring, whose branches climb over a wall. With bitterness archers attacked him; they shot at him with hostility. But his bow remained steady, his strong arms stayed limber, because of the hand of the Mighty One of Jacob, because of the Shepherd, the Rock of Israel, because of your father's God, who helps you, because of the Almighty, who blesses you with blessings of the heavens above, blessings of the deep that lies below, blessings of the breast and womb. Your father's blessings are greater than the blessings of the ancient mountains, than the bounty of the age-old hills. Let all these rest on the head of Joseph, on the brow of the prince among his brothers. "Benjamin is a ravenous wolf; in the morning he devours the prey, in the evening he divides the plunder."

Ge 48:14 But Israel reached out his right hand and put it on Ephraim's head, though he was the younger, and crossing his arms, he put his left hand on Manasseh's head, even though Manasseh was the firstborn. Then he blessed Joseph and said, "May the God before whom my father Abraham and Isaac walked, the God who has been my shepherd all my life to this day, the Angel who has delivered me from all harm —may he bless these boys. May they be called by my name and the names of my father Abraham and Isaac, and may they increase greatly upon the earth."

Now the descendants of St. KP Panggabean were continue by the birth of Isaac. Isaac was son of the fifth son, Giat, who likes Joseph son of Rachel, for he has protected the family. Isaac was the promised grandson of St. KP Panggabean. Therefore he must be the head of Israel for the next generation to protect, and to feed them all. He was some kind like

Ephraim, the son of Joseph who blessed by Jacob for Joseph had been feed the Israelites. But when the fourth son has his own son, he had to divided the firstborn bless into his descendants to be the king of Israel; i.e: King David, King Solomon, Daniel, Caleb, Jesus Christ the King of all kings (Gen. 49:8; Mt. 1:1-17) and bless Isaac as the bless of Ephraim (Gen.48:14), the bless of prosperity to feed the Israelites, and also Joshua, to lead and keep secure the God's people. The covenant friendship between God the Almighty, Jehovah, with St. KP Panggabean is the everlasting covenant relationship; a continual covenant friendship between God and St. KP Panggabean and his descendants: his seven children, his grandson Isaac, and their descendants throughout generation to come. They have to keep the covenant with God and obey to follow the law of the covenant, not to intermarry with Pagan but worship God. For God have chosen St. KP Panggabean in order that he will direct his children and his household after him to keep the way of the LORD by doing what is right and just, so that the LORD will bring about for St. KP Panggabean what he has promised him (Gen. 18:19). Any pagan male in their descendants, he will be cut off from his people; for he has broken God's covenant (Gen 17:14). They have to keep the covenant in Gen 18:19 and commandment in Dt 30:2-3: and when you and your children return to the LORD your God and obey him with all your heart and with all your soul according to everything I command you today, then the LORD your God will restore your fortunes and have compassion on you and gather you again from all the nations where he scattered you. (Dt.30:5-10) God will bring you to the land that belonged to your fathers, and you will take possession of it. He will make you more prosperous and numerous than your fathers. The LORD your God will circumcise your hearts and the hearts of your descendants, so that you may love him with all your heart and with all your soul, and live. The LORD your God will put all these curses on your enemies who hate and persecute you. You will again obey the LORD and follow all his commands I am giving you today. Then the LORD your God will make you most prosperous in all the work of your hands and in the fruit of your womb, the young of your livestock and the crops of your land. The LORD will again delight in you and make you prosperous, just as he delighted in your fathers, if you obey the LORD your God and keep his commands and decrees that are written in this Book of the Law and turn to the LORD your God with all your heart and with all your soul. In short they have to obey the Ten Commandment and the Book of the Law in order that they remain in the Covenant between God and their father St. KP Panggabean. And they have to keep the God's promise as their comfort in Daniel 12:3, "those who are wise will shine like the brightness of the heavens, and those who lead many to righteousness, like the stars forever and ever".

Wuhan Pandemic 2020-2022

In 2020 Wuhan lockdown due to outbreak Corona viruses. The virus has been transmitted to the world. In July 2021, Anna and Sudung positively suffered covid-19. The virus has been transmitted also to Giat, his wife and Isaac. Ruslan cries a lot for Anna. She says she doesn't wanna lose Anna. At night Sudung had three dreams in suffering the infection in three nights. At first night He has a dream he had been strangled by a big man and hard to breath. In next day he has a dream bitten by a snake. And in the next day he has a dream to meet three hungry wolves which are ready to pounch him. When he wakes up from the first dream, he does not bother with the first dream. When he has the second dreams, he begins to afraid of dying. And when he has the third dream, he understands the message of the dreams. He feels his last day is coming. He surrenders and asks forgiveness from God and promises he will do good things when he recover from his illness.

In the midst of Pandemic years Ruslan has suffered cyst in her kidney. She must has a treatment in hospital. Sudung accompanies her in hospital. After she had a treatment in hospital she cannot sleep in three days and night. Theo and Anes visit her. Theo: "Have you meet with the angels?" Ani: "Sister, why you ask Mom that?" Theo: "We have a lot of experience when grandad, grandma, Aunt Ready and Father in their last days. They have meet with the angels before they passed away". Ruslan: "I have seen Jesus. I have a theophany and meet Him. I also meet with your father, our forefather and foremother. They all have been gathered to welcome me." Ruslan finally breath her last and buried beside her husband. The whole church ministry visit her when she suffered illness. And The whole church ministry also come to visit her at her funeral. They all appreciate the work of her hands to planted the church. They say Ruslan has great hospitality. She will say greeting at first time when she sees her collegues. She acts like Abraham who has a great hospitality.

Question for reflection

1. Do the Bible story is truth? Proved!
2. Do the biblical story is historical? Proved!
3. How did God reveal and introduce himself to humankind?
4. How did God relate to humankind?
5. How did God save his people?

Reference

St KP Panggabean, Sejarah berdirinya HKBP Depok 2, 1994

O.P. Robertson, The Christ of the Covenants (Presbyterian and Reformed, 1980)

W.S. Prinsloo, "The Theology of the Book of Ruth," VT 30 (1980):330-41

Joseph Morecraft III, Covenant Lectures, Cassette recording

Holy Bible NIV, Zondervan